CRAFTED

A COMPENDIUM OF CRAFTS: NEW, OLD AND FORGOTTEN

Publishing Director Sarah Lavelle
Editor Harriet Butt
Designer Maeve Bargman
Illustrator Louise Lockhart
Production Director Vincent Smith
Production Controller Tom Moore

Published in 2019 by Quadrille, an imprint of Hardie Grant Publishing
Quadrille
52-54 Southwark Street
London SE1 1UN
quadrille.com

Cataloguing in Publication Data: a catalogue record for this book is available
from the British Library.

text © Sally Coulthard 2019
illustration © Louise Lockhart 2019
design © Quadrille 2019

ISBN 978 1 78713 256 6

Printed in China

CRAFTED

A COMPENDIUM OF CRAFTS:
NEW, OLD AND FORGOTTEN

SALLY COULTHARD

Illustrated by Louise Lockhart

Hardie Grant

QUADRILLE

FOR DAD,
a true craftsman

**'MAKING
IS THINKING'**

RICHARD SENNETT

CONTENTS

WOOD, WILLOW & NATURE

METAL

THE CULTURE
OF CRAFT

THE CULTURE OF CRAFT

People make things. Constantly. Compulsively. It seems we just can't help ourselves. Whether it's early humans smashing cobbles into cutting tools or Napoleonic sailors carving miniature ships from scavenged bones, the drive to create is one of our most defining and cherished traits.

But humans are also pragmatic. They like to create things with a purpose, a use. Throughout history, people have invented, perfected and shared these different techniques – from making paper to weaving baskets – so that today, we have a world culture that's rich with craft in all its different forms.

This is a book that celebrates the history, breadth and skill of crafts and the people who practice them. By delving into the origins of a craft, you often take unexpected turns or find connections between artisans; you see cultures developing their own versions of a particular craft, or spreading knowledge through trade or conflict. When you take the long view, it also becomes clear just how many crafts are endangered or have been lost. At other times, you find new crafts springing up in unexpected places, the result of new technologies or fresh-eyed artisans working at the boundaries of their skills.

Making stuff is at the very heart of who we are. One of the biggest leaps we made, on our evolutionary journey to become modern humans, was the discovery that we could make tools. Simple ones at first – just a few stone flakes chipped from a larger rock – but the advantage it gave us was a game-changer. Over 2.5 million years ago, these little stone cutters and scrapers gave our ape-like ancestors the upper hand over primates, allowing us to adapt and thrive in all sorts of new environments. Without *Homo habilis* ('skilled or handy man') we could have never evolved into *Homo sapiens* ('wise man').

It's an almost unimaginable distance between then and now, but the importance of making things hasn't diminished. There might be little, on the face of it, that links a village hall craft fair and one of the major leaps in human development, but at their heart the same, elegantly simple urge is playing itself out; the human desire to create something useful.

WHAT IS CRAFT?

At the beginning of any discussion about craft, it's useful to unpick what we mean. What is 'craft' exactly and how does a crafted object differ from, say, a piece of art or a factory-made thing? Perhaps the best place to start is to try and pin down a definition.

Craft is usually described as an activity or trade that uses a certain set of skills, usually manual. That's fine in as far as it goes, but it's missing out so much of the rich detail and nuance of craft. In his brilliant book, *Why We Make Things* and *Why It Matters*, furniture maker Peter Korn posits 'when it comes to definition, craft is a moving target.'

What he means is that the definition of craft *changes* depending on who you speak to and when; what a medieval person thought of as craft will not be equivalent to, say, someone in the 19th century. It is the same with how we view craftspeople. Today, the term is considered a compliment, a recognition of skill and status; not so for an ancient Egyptian slave, weaving in a cramped workshop or the 20th-century Ethiopian Jewish potter, viewed as an 'outcast' because her work involves fire and danger. According to Korn, craft is a 'conversation flowing through time'.

But just because craft is a fluid concept, it doesn't mean we shouldn't try to unravel some of its threads. If you and I had a chat about 'craft' on a street corner, I suspect we'd *broadly* agree, without having to say it, what we were talking about, so let's explore the idea a bit further.

One idea about craft is that the intention is different from, say, art. With art, the maker usually wants to say something abstract or meaningful with the object he or she is producing. The object's use is secondary. With craft, it's usually the other way round. The maker is setting out to craft something functional and useful, first and foremost, whether it's a pot, a rug or a horseshoe. If it says something profound or is beautiful to look at, that's an added bonus. There are always exceptions and shades of grey – and the art versus craft debate is a well-trodden road. The answer, for me, is that art and craft are like red and orange. Different yet similar. Separate and yet difficult to separate. It's more a question of emphasis.

There's also a sense that a craft needs a specialist set of skills, ones that are learned, practised and improved on; craft is often acquired through apprenticeship and training, whereas artists, by contrast, might rely on innate talent. The reality is that there is plenty of natural talent and self-guidance in craft while many artistic skills need to be taught, but again, it's a matter of degrees and perception.

People who have mastered a particular craft are respected. The words 'artisan' or 'craftsperson' are used to denote a level of sophistication or practical artistry, even when it comes to food. You can't walk down a high street without spotting someone selling craft beer or artisan bread. What's more, these skills can be passed down from generation to generation. Craft isn't lost if there's someone to receive the baton – it's handed on, added to and improved. That's how we evolved from carving stone tools to Corinthian columns. It's the accretion of culture.

Craft skills are also predominantly manual. Crafters make things by hand. While machines can be used to help in the process (a potter's wheel, for example, or a letterpress) there's an understanding that craft is essentially about practical handiwork, turning raw materials into objects using hand tools and physical dexterity. It's a moot point as we hurtle towards a future with greater mechanisation and digital content, whether craft will follow suit and rely less on handiwork. What's clear is that, when you make things by hand (as opposed to using a machine with predetermined settings) you are relying on the maker to get it right, not the machine. David Pye, craftsman and writer, wrestled with the problem in *The Nature and Art of Workmanship*; 'If I must ascribe meaning to the word craftsmanship, I shall say as a first approximation that it means simply workmanship using any kind of technique or apparatus, in which the quality of the result is not predetermined, but depends on the judgement, dexterity, and care which the maker exercises as he works.'

This careful handcrafting gives objects their other essential quality - uniqueness. While crafters can produce objects that look very similar – a potter can produce thousands of a single plate design – each is subtly different. The factory process, on the other hand, produces deliberately uniform objects. That's great if you're making technical components or items that need to be precise and identical, but the strength of craft is in its *essential humanity*, with all its delicious flaws and quirks.

Each crafted object says something about the person who made it. The maker may leave his or her mark deliberately by signing a piece, or through a particular flourish or technique that's unique to them. Either way, each craft object is as unique as the human who crafted it. It's an idea Richard Sennett championed in *The Craftsman*; that even 'anonymous workers can leave traces of themselves in inanimate things.'

Perhaps where things get a bit more muddled is our current use of the word 'craft' to cover everything from fine furniture to glitter-and-glue parties. The word has lost focus. We understand lots of different things when we talk about 'craft', from Fuzzy Felt to exquisite marquetry. It's a word that's simultaneously come to signify things that are expertly handmade and amateurishly homemade.

So, for the purpose of this book, there's an extra element to many of the crafts included: the idea of professionalism and quality. This is not a new notion. Cult classics such as Robert M. Pirsig's *Zen and the Art of Motorcycle Maintenance* explore the age-old adage that 'if a job's worth doing, it's worth doing properly' and it's an idea that pops up time and time again in discussions about craft. Richard Sennett comes to the conclusion that, for

him, 'the essence of craft is doing a job well for its own sake', while master carpenter Ole Thorstensen, in his reflections *Making Things Right*, concludes 'I would like to be judged on the basis of my profession, as though the profession itself is a person. So my notion of the competent craftsman appraising the quality of my work at some future date is very personal. I think a lot of the men who were builders more than a hundred years ago thought the same way. We form a long line of co-workers, friends almost, in my head.'

DOES CRAFT MATTER?

Is it important that we engage with the act of making things? If you've picked up this book there's a good chance that craft is important to you or someone you know. If you do any kind of craft you'll already know how satisfying, pleasurable, relaxing and infuriating making stuff can be.

On a personal level, the process of being creative and making something by hand involves using parts of my brain that other work can't reach. When you craft something, there's an intimate conversation that goes on between brain, eyes, body and hands, an exchange that's often totally instinctive and unselfconscious. You can lose hours, without noticing it; it's like meditating without trying.

When you make things by hand, there's also dialogue between you and the materials. All your senses are brought into play. Your tools become an extension of self; they're your allies, helping you reach your goal. There's often an economy of effort and movement that comes from a real familiarity with the task, tools and processes. How you treat your tools says something about the value you place on your craft. It teaches you to care for things, to recognise the importance of quality and organisation. 'My tools are an extension of me', writes Ole Thorstensen, 'by treating them with care I show the respect I have for the profession, the work, and for myself.'

My father spent his working life in adult education, creating learning opportunities for men and women. School had often let them down first time round, or they'd had to leave early to go into employment, and this was their second chance to do something creative and life-changing. Given the choice about which courses to offer students, Dad would always fight for high-quality craft workshops. What was the point, he thought, of spending an hour learning how to make knitted toilet-roll covers when you could be mastering the intricacies of dovetail joints or fine jewellery making? For him, learning craft is like taking a bus ride; once you've got on the bus, you might as well travel the whole route. It's no coincidence that Dad's mother had her own successful tailoring business, so he grew up seeing her being very precise about the standards of materials and workmanship she expected. It's also brilliant that, after early retirement, Dad decided to immerse himself in craft and fine furniture – putting into practice all the things that he'd learned over his career and finally expressing a side of himself that is absolutely core to his being.

Learning about, and practising, a craft has so many benefits, both for the individual and wider society. When you study craft, you gain a better appreciation of the 'culture of making' across a vast expanse of history and geography; when you experience craft, both at the design stage and in the making, you learn how to reflect critically on other people's work and, hopefully, your own. Craft is about problem solving, thinking creatively, looking for intelligent answers and trying new techniques; when you make things yourself you have a better understanding of the quality and value of other made things – it makes you a more discerning customer and consumer.

Playing with materials and developing an understanding of them gives you a more sophisticated grasp of aesthetics, construction and finish; crafting hones your practical and intellectual skills; you understand more about materials, tools and processes; and, best of all, taking part in a craft exercises different social skills – sharing, working alone, collaborating – not to mention being hugely pleasurable and mentally fulfilling.

Craft is a vital part of society and we must treasure and protect its status, especially in education. It challenges conventional ideas of what makes a whole, well-rounded person. In an interview, for BBC Radio 4's Desert Island Discs, comedian Jack Dee talked about his frustration at his school's emphasis on one type of knowledge; 'Some people have the talent of being able to absorb textbooks and then reproduce them in an exam. That's a wonderful gift to have. But there are other people who can create amazing pieces of furniture. Now, who's the more intelligent?'

THE CRAFT COMMUNITY

While governments may not currently recognise the value of craft as an essential part of society and wellbeing, it's interesting that people in the wider community are already way ahead of the game. While there's been a noticeable drop in the emphasis put on all kinds of art, design and craft in the national curriculum, there has been an explosion of craft classes and online tutorials, maker spaces, community events and craft sharing on social media. The creative industry as a whole is also one of the fastest growing sectors of both the US and the UK's general economy.

The statistics are hugely encouraging. Not only is craft cool – crafters are younger than the average population – but when it comes to gender, craft is increasingly blind. Half of all painters, illustrators, woodcrafters are men. And they also make up a third of all knitters. In the same breath, women are increasingly taking up traditionally male craft occupations, becoming blacksmiths, woodworkers, bookbinders and printers.

The common perception used to be that anyone interested in craft tended to stick to one discipline – not anymore. Research recently conducted in the US found that at least two-thirds of the population do at least one craft, but a quarter enjoy five or more. What's more, the same study showed that 9 out of 10 crafters spent five hours a week making stuff, while 4 out of 10 spend more than 20 hours a week. That's *half* a working week.

And it's not just hobbycraft. There's been a noticeable resurgence in commercial crafters (or micro-manufacturers, as they're sometimes called) and online platforms where people can sell their products. Success stories such as Etsy demonstrate how popular making and buying craft has become, whether it's someone crafting from a rural cottage or a makers' collective in an urban centre. The 'maker movement' is helping craft become a viable source of income thanks to shared maker spaces where creative people can meet, collaborate and produce goods using shared equipment or low-cost facilities.

MAKER SPACES

'Maker spaces' are gyms for crafters. They are places where you can go, exercise your creative muscles and experiment with different techniques and equipment. They are also places to meet like-minded people. Lots of crafts involve specialised or heavy machinery – pottery kilns, hot studios for glassmaking, cutting equipment, metal furnaces, etc – and getting access to these kinds of facilities has been tricky in the past. Previously the only option was to enrol on a course or evening class, in order to take advantage of an institution's craft amenities.

The beauty of maker spaces is their open access and lack of prescribed activities; if you have an idea, you can go and turn it into a reality on your own terms. There's also an attractive philosophy behind maker spaces – a sense of a wide community with a shared vision – so it's a kind of democratisation of making. To find a 'community centre with tools' near you, start with *spaces.makerspace.com*, a vast international directory of maker spaces.

The craft community is wide and generous. There are dozens of people who'd be thrilled to talk to you about their craft, show you more, teach you things or suggest new ideas. If you've got a craft you want to share, there are now lots of ways to do it. If you're shy, social media is a great place to start as you're in control and the communication is at a distance. If you're confident about public speaking, teach a class or start an informal club. As Einstein famously said, 'Creativity is infectious. Pass it on.'

Thankfully there's no longer the imperative to choose between being a crafter and following a conventional career path. Work patterns are changing. People are supporting themselves via different, numerous income streams, one or more of which may be craft related. This idea of 'side hustles' – or small business ideas that bring in extra income on top of your day job – is growing; not only does it allow you to set up a new venture without taking huge financial risks, but it also gets away from the idea of you having to define your life by one narrow career choice. Why not be an insurance broker *and* a bookbinder? Who says you can't teach maths *and* earn money as a hand-knitter?

What's clear is that people are hungry for craft and are finding their own ways to learn, train, collaborate and get making. It seems you can't keep a good crafter down.

BUYING AND DISPLAYING CRAFT

If you care about craft, as well as reading up about it, one of the best ways to demonstrate your support is to buy hand-crafted objects. All too often we moan about the lack of quality or care taken over a mass-produced item and yet we struggle with the idea of spending more to own something made by a craftsperson. Even if you're not a maker yourself, there are plenty of reasons to fill your home with craft. Not only are you helping to boost your regional economy, reduce the carbon footprint of goods and support small local businesses, but the best bit about buying craft is living in an environment filled with beautifully made objects.

We have a subtle and important relationship with the furniture, homewares and ornaments we surround ourselves with. Our choices say something about us, what our tastes are, and what kind of people we'd like to be. As Alain de Botton wrote in *The Architecture of Happiness*, 'While keeping us warm and helping us in mechanical ways [works of design and architecture] simultaneously hold out an invitation for us to be specific sorts of people. They speak visions of happiness.'

These objects also talk back to us, telling us something about the people who made them. A flat-pack wardrobe will communicate very little, but a hand-thrown pot or carved wooden spoon speaks volumes about the maker. If you are lucky enough to know the craftsperson, every time you touch or look at the object it will remind you of them, a memory of a workshop visit or the moment you bought the piece. Buying craft is often addictive; one object can often lead to another or take you on a sideways journey into a new discipline. Through one crafter you may meet another. Through one precious object you may find dozens of others.

ENDANGERED CRAFTS

The modern world can be a difficult place for a craftsperson. While lots of crafts are in rude health, there are a significant number of traditional skills that are in danger of disappearing altogether. Many of these crafts are hundreds, if not thousands, of years old, and make up the fabric of our material culture. From dry stone walls to clog making, basket weaving to coach building, lots of these time-honoured crafts are at risk of dying out due to lack of apprentices coming into the trade or the effect of cheaper, mass-produced goods.

Some people might argue that losing traditional crafts is just a natural function of a changing world. If we don't need rake makers, then why worry whether they still practise their craft or not? But here's the thing: many other areas of traditional life are cherished and preserved, not because they are particularly useful to us, but because their presence adds to the richness of our living environment. We value period buildings, for example, even after their original use may have changed or they've fallen into disrepair. These old structures link us to the near past, providing context and continuity in a fast-paced world. The same principle applies to

traditional crafts; they're a living link to our heritage and a skill-set that, if lost and not recorded, would be very difficult to revive.

It would be wrong to assume these heritage crafts are obsolete, however. In many cases, the few crafters that do continue to practice a particular trade are often rushed off their feet, with waiting lists months long and an impatient customer base. Heritage crafts are a vital part of the maintenance and upkeep of our traditional landscape and buildings. We need lime plasterers to repair our ancient buildings, dry stone wallers to rebuild field boundaries, and marblers to produce exquisite papers for the bookbinding trade. Cricket bat makers, lead workers, coopers – so many of these heritage crafts are woven into the fabric of our cultural identity. They also contribute a significant amount to the economy.

Craft is rarely practised in isolation. Crafters talk to each, compare notes, share techniques and trade secrets. The skills of traditional craftspeople are useful to modern crafters in so many ways. Not only can they teach us about their own craft but their approaches to materials, work practices and tools are all things modern crafters can learn from.

There is reason to be hopeful. Many people recognise the importance of traditional crafts and have come up with ways to protect them. Organisations such as the UK's Heritage Crafts Association (HCA) and United Nations Educational, Scientific and Cultural Organization (UNESCO) work to safeguard and promote traditional craft skills through strategies such as research, advocacy and access to training and bursaries. Success will depend on a number of factors, not least getting more young creatives trained in traditional crafts. People also need to bolster heritage crafts, either by buying or commissioning craft goods, and also supporting heritage-based institutions, such as The National Trust or English Heritage, who employ traditional craftspeople as part of their ongoing business.

But beyond the rational, economic argument, there's something to be said about crafts and their place in our consciousness. There's obviously something significant going on here because craft-related things seem to strike a chord with people. They look at exhibitions, love demonstrations and buy craft products. So something is clearly satisfying a need.

Onlookers want to see traditional crafts being practised because it helps them understand a bit about where they, themselves, came from. Most will have stories in their families about someone who made shoes or hats or baked bread or was a cabinet maker. Seeing the thing being done is to feel a direct link with a different way of living that's more deeply rooted than mere nostalgia.

Preserving old skills meets a consistent need. We seem to want to preserve expertise and see it in action. We've all been to see crafters in action – blacksmiths, gilders, bookbinders, boat makers, potters, clog makers, glassblowers, carpenters and so on – often in the company of other people who are also clearly fascinated. Modern life often insulates us from the acts of creation which used to be commonplace. We seem to like being in the company of someone making stuff.

Our definition of what is beautiful also overlaps with handmade, traditional objects. There is something intrinsically whole and good about a simple object made skilfully, especially when you get the sense that the thing itself, and the way it was made, come from years of *really* knowing a particular material. We must keep practising old craft skills because it's important to see them happen and handmade things speak to us like no manufactured object can.

From the perspective of the crafter, they want to be involved in traditional crafts for all kinds of reasons. For some, they can't *not* do it; it's been a passion for ages, a skill they've always had in some form, maybe a family member did it before. Others share the view about the beauty of handmade objects and it's a constant (almost) source of pleasure to be active in that world. Others makers see much of modern life as hostile to individual action and want affirmation that they exist in their own right and have some freedoms that they can really exercise. Each craft object a person makes reminds them that they exist as a skilled, separate person and that, good or bad, success or failure, it's down to them alone. That's rare in the world of work.

CAN YOU MAKE A LIVING FROM CRAFT?

The short answer is yes. The more complicated answer is that to make craft pay you need to follow some strict rules. It's an irritating cliché that creative people can't be business-minded. For thousands of years, craftspeople have supported themselves, their families and their communities through their work; the key, without sounding trite, is to take it seriously. Ask any committed crafter and they'll tell you the same few things:

1 Never Stop Learning

To succeed, you always need to keep learning, improving and developing as a crafter. Read widely around your craft, keep absorbing and refining new skills, be aware of trends, visit exhibitions and other crafters in your field. And get some basic business skills, whether that's by taking a short course or teach yourself. At the end of the day, making a living from craft is as much about selling as it is making.

2 Be Open to Other Income Streams

Craft businesses, like any other, fluctuate and can be particularly prone to recessions, when people stop spending on 'non-necessities'. Many crafters find it useful to have other related strings to their bow – teaching, workshops, writing, etc. You may also need to structure your craft business so that the less interesting, but profitable, bread-and-butter work brings in enough income to support the more creative, personal projects.

3 Know Your Worth

There's a huge temptation to undervalue your craft, pricing your products so they'll sell quickly. While it's important to be realistic about what the buying public will pay, it's also vital that you factor in your time, skill, outgoings, training and material costs. Craft can never compete with mass-market goods and shouldn't try to. Underselling your craft also doesn't do fellow crafters any favours – it sets a dangerous precedent.

4 Develop Relationships

People buy craft because they want to engage with the crafter. That relationship is hugely important to your business. You may find that you have a handful of loyal clients who provide a disproportionately large amount of your sales. Cultivate these relationships. Keep in touch. Invite clients to viewings and maker days. Make it clear what they're buying into – individuality, uniqueness, sustainability, heritage, local business and the joy of the handmade – only *you* can make the things you make.

PAPER, PEN
& PRINT

PAPERMAKING

Cai Lun was a Chinese eunuch working in the court of Emperor He at the beginning of the 2nd century A.D. Legend has it that, one day, he was idly watching wasps making their nests. Intrigued by the way the buzzing insects chewed up bits of fibrous plants to make pulp, which then dried to a stiff, paper-like material, Cai Lun struck upon an idea.

Court officials had previously written on weighty bamboo tablets or expensive sheets of silk, so you can only imagine the Emperor's delight when, in A.D. 105, Cai Lun revealed his new, cheaper invention – paper. His technique, which involved mashing up bark, hemp, old rags and fishing nets, then sieving the resulting pulp and forming it into sheets, was an instant hit. It revolutionised writing and literacy throughout China.

The technique was closely guarded, however, and it took another thousand years for the craft of papermaking to reach European shores. Paper was traded throughout the East, along the Silk Route, but it wasn't until a handful of Chinese papermakers were captured by Arab troops after a battle in 751 that the secrets of paper manufacture finally arrived in the Middle East. From there, the knowledge spread to North Africa, and finally, during the Crusades, across into Spain at the end of the 11th century. The first paper mill in England didn't open until 1495.

What's fascinating is that, although two millennia have passed since Cai Lun's discovery, handmade paper is still produced in roughly the same way – by turning fibre into pulp into paper. Papermakers today still use old cloth rags, plant material or scrap paper as their raw materials. These are broken down into a thick papery soup – either by pounding, beating or blending the raw materials with water – before being formed into a sheet. This is done using a screened frame (called a mould and deckle) which sieves the fibres out of the watery pulp, before being tipped onto an absorbent surface (a process called couching), pressed and left to dry.

|||||||||||||||||||||||||||||||||||||||||||||||||||||||||||||||||||

DID YOU KNOW?

The word 'paper' is actually older than the thing it describes. Paper comes from the Ancient Greek 'papuros' and refers to papyrus, a thick paper-like material made from the plant of the same name, used for at least two and half thousand years before true paper was invented.

|||||||||||||||||||||||||||||||||||||||||||||||||||||||||||||||||||

The legacy of Cai Lun lives on in China today, but it's interesting that recent archaeological discoveries suggest that people may have been experimenting with papermaking hundreds of years earlier than we first thought. At Fangmatan, a burial site in China's Gansu Province, a body was found with the remains of a paper map laid on his chest. Only fragments survived but the tomb dates from 179–41 B.C., making these paper scraps the oldest ever found, pre-dating Cai Lun's invention by around two hundred years.

PAPIER MÂCHÉ

Almost as soon as the Chinese had invented paper, they began to explore its possibilities as a material. They swiftly discovered that when paper pulp or strips of paper were mixed with an adhesive, such as glue or resin, it could be moulded into shapes that, once dry, were extraordinarily robust. Given extra coats of waterproof lacquer, the possible uses of this material were endless.

Some of the earliest examples of papier mâché are soldiers' helmets and pot lids from China's Han Dynasty (206 B.C.-A.D. 220) and a tiny coffin, commissioned by a Persian nobleman for his favourite falcon. The material was both popular and versatile, it was cheaper to make than plaster and, when lacquered with layers of resin, it was tough enough to be treated like wood.

Since then, papier mâché has been used for everything from masks to canoes, trays to children's toys. In 1853 *The Illustrated London News* even ran a story about a full-size papier mâché village, created for a wealthy man relocating to Australia. His papier mâché village included ten houses, ranging from two to six bedrooms, and a vast storehouse. 'The material of the several houses is a patent waterproof, papier mâché,' enthused the journalist.

'It consists of paper and rags, beautifully ground and reduced to pulp, which, when dry and pressed, become as hard as a board.' Even the mantelpieces were made from papier mâché.

Interestingly, although the words papier mâché mean 'chewed paper', the phrase didn't originate in France. The name probably comes from French immigrants who worked in London's papier mâché factories during the mid 1700s. In a brilliantly unlikely story, one of its chief manufacturers, a Mr. Wilton of Cavendish Square, London, is said to have employed two French women to frantically chew paper in the days before the factory switched to using machines for the process, hence the name.

PAPER QUILLING

If you were a young lady of means in the late 1700s or early 1800s, you could have done worse than learn the art of paper quilling. Along with EMBROIDERY (pages 96-99), paper quilling (also called paper filigree), was *the* pastime for accomplished women, described at the time by *New Lady's Magazine* as 'the art which affords an amusement to the female mind capable of the most pleasing and extensive variety.' It even gets a mention in Jane Austen's *Sense and Sensibility*:

'Perhaps,' continued Elinor, 'if I should happen to cut out, I may be of some use to Miss Lucy Steele, in rolling her papers for her; and there is so much still to be done to the basket, that it must be impossible, I think, for her labour singly, to finish it this evening.'

It's a genteel craft, one that involves rolling thin strips of paper around a feather quill (or something similar) to form spirals, which are then applied to surfaces as a form of decoration. Early practitioners were medieval monks and nuns, who used paper snipped from the gilded edges of books to create ornate designs for holy relics and religious panels. From a distance it would have mimicked more expensive gold and silver wirework filigree, a craft dating back as far as Ancient Egypt.

After the Protestant Reformation, many kinds of religious adornment fell out of favour. During the 18th century, however, quilling once again became a hit handicraft, this time with young ladies whose delicate dispositions, it was thought, would not be too taxed by the work. The paper filigree was often applied to small items – tea caddies, trays, boxes, cabinets, mirrors and screens. Even Henry VIII's daughter, Princess Elizabeth, joined the craze, commissioning a cabinet to be made so she could cover it in her own paper quills.

Far from being a forgotten art, paper quilling has become something of a cult craft. In recent years, new crafters such as Russia's Yulia Brodskaya have taken paper quilling to a new level of artistic expression, experimenting with formats such as quilled portraits and typography.

PAPER FOLDING

No-one knows who first folded paper, but China and Japan are both strong contenders. The Japanese have been folding paper for a long time, especially for religious ceremonies and rituals. Zigzag folded paper shapes called *shide* and butterflies are some of the earliest Japanese examples we know about and probably date back as far as the Heian period (A.D. 794–1185), while the Chinese funereal *yuanbao* – paper folded to look like gold nuggets – are equally ancient.

More unexpected, however, is how long paper folding has been floating around Europe. Some scholars put the date as early as the 1100s; there's early proof in the form of an illustration of a paper boat in a book called *De Sphaera Mundi (On the Sphere of the World)* dated 1490. In 1614, an English play mentions children playing with paper flytraps (what we now know as origami waterbombs), while napkin folding, which was hugely fashionable in aristocratic circles before 1600, used many of the same patterns and techniques as modern origami. Whether these techniques were picked up from foreign traders and travellers, or the traditions emerged independently, remains a mystery.

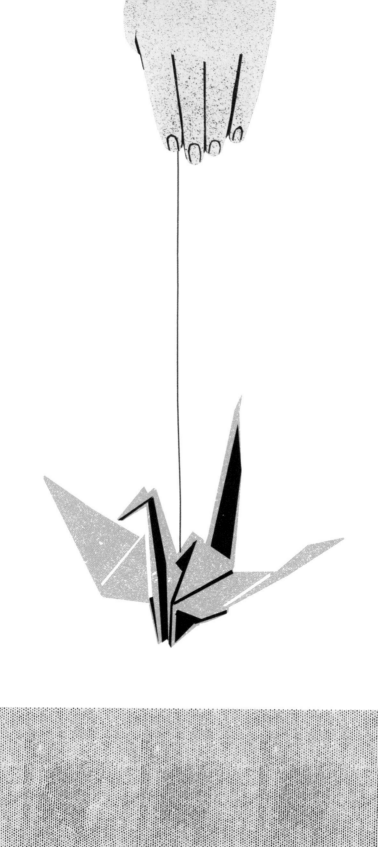

ORIGAMI

For hundreds of years, paper folding techniques were passed on verbally. The first written instructions didn't appear in Japan until 1797 with the publication of *Senbazuru Orikata (Thousand Crane Folding)*. This, combined with the accessibility of cheaper, mass-produced paper, helped turn the craft into a fashionable pastime. The term 'origami' was only coined in 1880, however, from the words *oru* (to fold) and *kami* (paper). Up until that point it was known as *orikata* (folded shapes) or *orisue* (folded setting down).

Modern origami owes a great deal to one man: Akira Yoshizawa. Considered the grandmaster of paper folding, in the 1950s Akira published *Atarashii Origami Geijutsu (New Origami Art)*. Together with American Sam Randlett, Akira developed a system for describing origami folds that's still used today. During his lifetime he published numerous books and made over 50,000 models, many of which he lent to exhibitions or gave away as gifts.

Origami is still wildly popular. Along with colouring books, adults have flocked to origami as a way to engage with a practical, challenging activity that doesn't revolve around technology. It's also thought to improve certain mental and spatial skills,

developing hand-eye coordination and mathematical reasoning. A recent TED talk by origamist Robert Lang, who mixes maths, science and origami to produce folds once thought of as impossible, has been viewed more than 2.3 million times.

PAPER MODELLING

It's a short leap from origami to paper modelling. While in origami you create a 3D shape without cutting or gluing, paper modelling isn't as prescriptive, allowing you to make scale models using stiff paper or card, which is cut out, scored, folded and stuck together.

Paper modelling is a craft that's both pleasingly traditional and cutting edge. Some of the earliest paper models designed to be cut out and assembled can be found in French toy catalogues from the 1800s. The craze soon spread to Germany and the UK. Victorian and Edwardian children delighted in models of farmhouses, circus tents, dolls, famous landmarks, modes of transport and theatres. These paper models not only gave children an opportunity to hone practical skills, but the models – made by manufacturers such as Pellerin in France and Milton Bradley in the US – also provided glimpses of impossibly exotic countries and ways of life.

PEPAKURA

The pleasure of turning a flat 2D image into a tangible 3D model hasn't diminished, even with the rise of digital technology. Pepakura, a modern offshoot of paper modelling, uses a computer program to turn 3D data – such as a digital model of a suit of armour – into a flat, buildable template. The template is then printed off on a home printer, cut out, folded and glued together.

PAPER CUTTING

It's impossible to pinpoint when paper cutting began. Paper doesn't survive well in the archaeological records, but the knowledge that the Chinese had access to both paper and scissors from around A.D. 200 (see CRAFT INVENTIONS, pages 74-75), suggests that someone must have, soon after this time, had the bright idea to start snipping.

There are some wonderful early examples of paper cutting. A beautiful geometric circle, dating from around the 4th or 5th century A.D., was discovered in China. Another paper cut – a chain of people holding hands – was found in a grave in Jixjiang, dating back to the Tang Dynasty (A.D. 618-907). What's interesting is that, although the objects themselves are old, the designs are even older, suggesting that the custom of cutting out figures, flowers or landscapes (from other materials such as silk or hemp) may be hundreds if not thousands of years older. Some patterns are symbolic – wishing for a long life or healing, for example – while others represent famous folk tales or scenes from everyday life.

Traditionally, paper cutting was women's work. A folk art passed on from mother to daughter, the craft is still viewed as one of China's major cultural pastimes. But it also holds special significance for many other cultures: the Jewish have a long and rich heritage of paper cutting, both religious and decorative, while more recently, European countries including Poland, Sweden, Germany and the Netherlands have developed intricate, lace-like traditions of their own. Today, paper cutting is enjoying something of a revival, thanks in part, to a fresh interest in folk art and Scandinavian traditions. Rather than slavishly copying ancient designs, however, a new wave of paper cutters, such as Rob Ryan and Nikki McClure, are working in innovative ways, incorporating words into designs or exploring political and social ideas through the medium.

DÉCOUPAGE

One of the most incredible discoveries in recent years was the burial tombs of an ancient nomadic tribe who lived in the Altai Mountains in Siberia, 400 years before the birth of Christ. The frozen landscape preserved many of the objects in the tombs, which would have otherwise rotted away over time, including the world's oldest example of découpage. The Pazyryk people, it turns out, were incredible craftspeople, especially skilled with FELT and LEATHER, which they cut into shapes and stuck onto the tombs of their dead. Archaeologists found cut-out images of lions, goats, reindeer and many other exquisite designs, as well as early examples of APPLIQUÉ and WEAVING.

The word découpage comes from the French *découper* (to cut out), but again it seems that Europe arrived late to the party. China and Japan had been covering objects with paper and lacquer (see PAPIER MÂCHÉ, pages 32–33) for hundreds of years before the late 1600s, when Oriental lacquered furniture became highly fashionable in Europe. Supply couldn't meet demand and so Italian craftsmen began to produce their own 'fake' lacquerwork to keep up with the public's appetite; prints and engravings would be hand-coloured, intricately cut out, pasted onto furniture and ornaments and given numerous layers of lacquer as a protective coat.

The trend for hand-colouring continued apace until the Victorian era when printing techniques and paper production revolutionised decorative papers. Sentimental greetings cards, heavily embossed papers and printed images became affordable and the perfect material to cut out and apply to every surface imaginable, including lamp stands, screens, hat boxes, trinkets and picture frames.

DECOPATCH

Découpage is still hugely popular, especially in the US, where the trend for upcycling has led to a fresh approach, more akin to collage. 'Decopatch' is a modern take on découpage. Originally a trade name for the company that makes the papers and adhesives, decopatch has become a generalised term for sticking tissue-like, pre-printed papers onto objects. The same product is used as both the glue and finishing lacquer, making the process quicker and easier.

MARBLING

The deeply satisfying craft of marbling probably originated in Japan in the 12th century. There, it was called *suminagashi* (ink floating), and involved dropping splashes of black or blue pigment onto the surface of a tray of water. The ink would then be blown into swirls and smoke-like patterns.

By the 15th century, Persia and Turkey had taken the technique and improved on it. Using oil paints and a thicker, viscous floating liquid meant that the marbler had a greater level of control over the patterns and spread of colour. Two hundred years later, via trade and travel, marbling arrived in Europe. Even today, many people call marbled paper 'Turkish Paper', a name that recognises how accomplished the Ottoman Empire was at producing exquisite designs.

It's a relatively simple process; patterns are made by floating inks onto the surface of water or a gelatinous liquid called 'size'. The inks are dropped in one after the other and then swirled around, feathered, combed or gently shaken in the tray to produce a marble-like design onto which a piece of paper is gently laid, lifted off and left to dry. No two patterns are ever alike and the beauty of marbling is often in its unexpected, organic results.

From the 17th century, marbled papers were highly prized both by collectors and bookbinders (see BOOKBINDING, pages 50–53), who would use the decorative sheets as book covers, endpapers or fore-edges. As well as being highly ornamental, marbled paper also had its practical uses. Marbled papers were sometimes used as a background for important documents, making them impossible to forge, while bookbinders found that marbled papers often disguised the wear and tear that plain book covers couldn't hide.

Despite its appeal, marbling is today counted as an ENDANGERED CRAFT (pages 21–25), with only a handful of marblers working at a professional level both in the US and across Europe. Fewer books are traditionally hand-bound, digital printing is ubiquitous, and there are few apprentices going into the craft. That said, the community of practising marblers is a close one and well represented by organisations such as US-based International Marbling Network, which provides information and lists of professional marblers not only in North and South America, but across Asia, Europe and Africa.

BOOKBINDING

The history of bookbinding is inextricably linked to the development of writing (see CALLIGRAPHY & ILLUMINATION, pages 56-59). From about 3000 B.C., people started to write things down – at first on wet clay tablets or carved into stone, but soon after on more portable materials such as papyrus, parchment (animal skin) or thin sheets of wood covered in wax. For works of any length, such as religious texts, scholars would write on scrolls that were then rolled up and stored in cylindrical containers.

One downside of a scroll is that you have to unroll the whole thing before you can read it. Tricky if you needed to refer to something in a hurry. The 'codex' or book (plural 'codices'), seem to have been developed by the Romans, who had the bright idea of stacking sheets of written material and binding them together, rather than writing on one long continuous roll.

Early examples include wooden writing tablets, hinged or lashed together (the word 'codex' comes from the Latin *caudex*, or tree trunk) and Roman notebooks made from parchment. The idea of the book caught on and quickly spread, thanks in part to early Christians who adopted the book as their preferred way of setting down the words of the newly written

||||||||||||||||||||||||||||||||||||||||||||||||||||||||||||||||||||||||||

DID YOU KNOW?

The word 'book' may come from an early German word *bokiz* or 'beech' and refer to the ancient practice of writing on tree bark. Curiously, the French equivalent *livre* comes from the Latin *librum*, meaning 'inner tree bark'.

||||||||||||||||||||||||||||||||||||||||||||||||||||||||||||||||||||||||||

Bible. By A.D. 500, books had all but replaced the use of scrolls throughout the Western world.

Interestingly, it seems that other cultures were developing similar ideas independently. The Mayan civilisation in Central America was also using codices to record astrological information and ritual knowledge. After Spanish conquistadores and missionaries burned all the indigenous written records in the mid 1500s, only a handful of these paper-bark books remain. What does survive tells us that Mayan people were making books perhaps even as early as A.D. 300.

Back in China, where papermaking was already well established, books didn't catch on initially. Even when sheets of paper were available, the Chinese preferred to paste them together to create long strips, which could then be rolled up into a scroll or folded, concertina style. Bookbinding, as we know it, didn't gain popularity in China until the Tang Dynasty (A.D. 618–907).

The earliest example of European bookbinding that survives is the Stonyhurst Gospel of St.John, a beautiful and miraculously well-preserved red leather-bound book that was made in the North East of England in the late 7th century

and placed in St. Cuthbert's coffin on the island of Lindisfarne. Despite its antiquity, this little book was crafted in ways instantly recognisable to modern bookbinders. In fact, industrial processes and digital printing may have changed the way most books are produced but hand-bound books still employ the same techniques, materials and tools used for centuries.

Binding techniques vary. Each method has its own wonderfully descriptive name – from 'Japanese stab' and 'medieval limp' to 'secret Belgian' and 'piano hinge' – but the essence of most is that papers are bound together along one edge, either sewn or glued, given a front and back cover for protection, and then decorated. Here, the bookbinder may draw on other crafters' skills, from gilding with gold leaf to stamping, silversmithing and leatherwork.

BOOK ART

Happily, bookbinding is a craft that's alive and well thanks to a steady supply of conservation and repair work to antiquarian books, volumes for libraries and museums, or special commissions such as family histories or one-off projects. But it would be a mistake to view bookbinding as a craft only relevant to historic volumes and restoration projects. Elaborate bookbindings may seem a little out of place in today's world of e-readers but the idea of the book as an 'object' – a thing of aesthetic value and beauty – is more popular than ever. Sometimes called 'book artists', there is a dynamic and hugely creative collection of bookbinders across the US and Europe, who regularly create and exhibit contemporary bindings. Rather than follow the conventions of traditional bookbinding – with its calf skin and gold tooling – these crafters often experiment with other materials such as beads, wire and fabric, to create book covers that are not only gloriously beautiful but also attempt to convey the work they enclose. One of the societies that organizes such events – the highly regarded Designer Bookbinders – also actively supports ten new binders each year to help continue the hand-binding tradition.

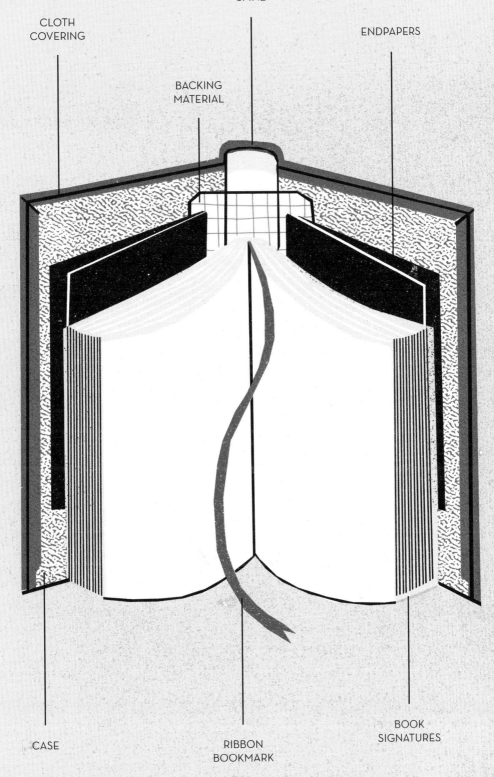

CLOTH COVERING

SPINE

ENDPAPERS

BACKING MATERIAL

CASE

RIBBON BOOKMARK

BOOK SIGNATURES

GLOBEMAKING

Contrary to popular belief, ancient civilisations didn't think the world was flat. Greek philosophers, working in the 5th century B.C., came up with the notion of the earth as a sphere surrounded by constellations of stars. The earliest celestial globe – showing the position of the stars – sits on the shoulders of the Farnese Atlas, a 2nd-century Roman marble statue, while Chinese records date their first celestial globe to between 70 and 50 B.C.

We don't know much, however, about the craft of globemaking before the 13th century. The Islamic World was also fascinated by astrology and a handful of metal celestial globes from this period have survived. The earliest known example was made in Muslim Spain in Valencia in 1080, while the British Museum holds an exquisite celestial globe from Mosul; made from brass inlaid with silver, it's thought to date from 1275. Other written evidence suggests globes being made from copper, wood, marble and even glass.

The earliest surviving globe of Earth, however, dates from 1492. The Martin Behaim globe from Nuremburg was constructed not from metal, but from a linen-based PAPIER MÂCHÉ, laminated for strength and covered with strips of parchment and painted. The 15th and 16th centuries were a period of rapid technological change and renewed scientific interest; travellers explored new worlds and globes became not only a scientific instrument but a symbol of learning. While earlier globes were crafted by silversmiths and engravers, with the invention of the PRINTING press in the mid-1450s, it became possible to print out paper maps that could be cut and pasted onto cheaper PAPIER MÂCHÉ or wooden spherical moulds. Globemaking changed from a metalworking craft to a craft for papermakers and printers.

Today, traditional globemakers are a rarity. Only two workshops worldwide still make handcrafted globes, including London-based Bellerby and Co., a company established not centuries ago, but in 2008 when founder Peter Bellerby couldn't find a globe for his father's 80th birthday and decided to make one himself by hand.

CALLIGRAPHY & ILLUMINATION

The word 'calligraphy' comes from the Greek *kallos* (beautiful or fine) and *graphein* (to write or draw) and is generally viewed as the art or craft of handwriting. Across the world, as far back as 5,000 years ago, ancient cultures developed their own system for writing things down. What's interesting is that taking the time to write beautifully, carefully and in a certain style, with rules about letter formation, was often reserved for religious texts; the sacred words were so important that they could only be done justice if they were written exquisitely and with artistry. It seems God, not the Devil, was in the detail.

The Arabs have a saying, 'Purity of writing is purity of the soul'. Master calligraphers had, and still have, an important status in Islamic society. Only persons of true spiritual devotion and clarity of faith, it's believed, can reach the level of talent needed for this most sacred of crafts.

A picture speaks a thousand words, however, so it wasn't long before many religious texts became illuminated. Handwritten books or scrolls would be embellished with exquisite paintings or decorated initials, vibrantly coloured and often gilded with gold leaf, the idea being that the page was literally enlightened or illuminated with decoration.

Before the advent of printing, all books were copied out by hand, including bibles. One of the most dazzling examples is the *Lindisfarne Gospels*, an illuminated manuscript thought to have been made by a monk, Eadfrith, beavering away in a monastery off the coast of Northumberland, England, around A.D. 700. There are thought to be over 90 colours used in his book. Few pigments would have been available to Eadfrith locally, so historians believe he must have sourced colours from as far away as the Mediterranean and, for blue lapis lazuli, the Himalayas.

The invention of the PRINTING press, in the middle of the 15th century, soon reduced the need for hand-copied books. It didn't spell the end for calligraphy and illumination, but rather it pushed the skills to a corner, where they languished for 400 years. Interest in calligraphy and medieval manuscripts was piqued by followers of William Morris and the Arts and Crafts movement at the end of the

1800s, who admired and copied ancient crafts. But it was Edward Johnston (1872–1944) who almost single-handedly revived the art of formal penmanship in his book *Writing and Illuminating, and Lettering*, first published in 1906 and never out of print since. Johnston, who initially read medicine, abandoned his studies to follow his passion for calligraphy. Whilst teaching Lettering and Illumination to students at the newly formed Central School of Arts and Crafts in London, Johnston began to pour over early medieval manuscripts in the British Museum and teach himself, and then others, techniques that had been lost for centuries. A brilliant calligrapher and letter designer, he also invented the eponymous 'sans-serif' typeface famously used across the London Underground.

One of the most interesting developments in calligraphy has been its recent and stratospheric rise in popularity thanks to the Instagram generation. Few things can be crafted quickly, but calligraphy ticks all the boxes when it comes to immediacy and instant appeal; short videos capture the movement and rhythm of hand lettering in a satisfyingly brief length of time.

Renowned calligraphers such as Russia's Artem Stepanov or the UK's Seb Lester, who has over a million followers, understand the innate appeal of watching something 'perfect' being created, by hand, from start to finish in just a few seconds. Calligraphy, of all the crafts, is also an endeavour that's managed to embrace new directions, without feeling compromised; modern calligraphers often talk about embracing imperfections and breaking traditional rules of lettering, to create handwriting that's more about energy and personality than slavish accuracy. At its extreme, calligraphy has even brushed shoulders with the world of graffiti – the New York-based artist Faust has taken fine penmanship to the new heights, for example, creating large-scale graffiti that blends classical calligraphy sensibilities with tragedy street art.

||||||||||||||||||||||||||||||||||||||||||||||||||||||||||||||

DID YOU KNOW?

The word manuscript comes from the medieval Latin *manuscriptus*, from manu (by hand) and *scriptus* (written).

||||||||||||||||||||||||||||||||||||||||||||||||||||||||||||||

BLOCK PRINTING

In 1994, three French cavers stumbled upon one of the most significant prehistoric sites to date. The Chauvet-Pont-d'Arc cave contains more than a thousand ancient paintings, dating from around 32,000 years ago. Amongst them are some of the oldest examples of printing ever known – handprints – made by early humans rubbing their hands in red ochre and pressing them on the cave wall.

Printing, as we understand it today, usually involves ink but the Chauvet cave demonstrates the elegant simplicity behind the idea – that it's possible to make an image, again and again, without having to draw it out by hand. Throughout history, people have explored this idea – using everything from cylindrical stamps carved from stone to halved potatoes – to print repeated images onto a surface.

Some of the earliest printed fabrics ever found include a textile fragment with a floral pattern from the Western Han Dynasty (206 B.C.–A.D. 9). Quite how the floral patterns were printed remains unsolved – possibly bronze stamps were used. Wood blocks, however, were cheaper and easier to carve, and it's no surprise that block printing became *the* method for printing fabric, and subsequently paper, across the Far East.

Written in 868 A.D., and hidden for centuries in a sealed cave in China, the Buddhist text *Diamond Sutra* is the world's earliest complete survival of a wooden block printed book.

Perhaps even more tantalising is bust of a king priest, found at Mohenjo-daro, in modern-day Pakistan. The statue dates from around 2000 B.C. but appears to be wearing a blockprinted shawl, very similar to the popular wooden block-printed ajrak cotton shawl still worn day, suggesting to scholars that block printing has been around for longer than we first imagined. India and Pakistan are still two of the largest makers and exporters of blockprinted fabric in the world, their carefully crafted work drawing the attention of modern British designers such as Vanessa Arbuthnott and Pooky lampshades.

Block printing also lends itself to wallpaper. John Houghton, writing in 1699, describes wallpaper in 'a great Variety, with curious Cuts [woodcuts]' which are 'very pritty, clean and will last with tolerable care a great while.' The nobility had long covered their castle walls with richly decorated tapestries but, for the ambitious merchant and middle class, fabric hangings were often too pricey, or too difficult to obtain from the mainland Europe. Wallpaper,

carefully blockprinted by skilled artisans, became a popular alternative and as Houghton wrote, an affordable way to make 'the houses of the more ordinary people look neat.'

Methods of printing wallpaper changed little until the beginning of the 1800s. The invention of machine printing, coupled with the repeal of excise duty on printed paper, suddenly made wallpaper even cheaper, bringing it within the reach of the Victorian working class. Its status as a method of decoration plummeted – from elite to everyman – with many of the designers and wealthy tastemakers of the day branding it vulgar and populist.

Today, wallpaper has wriggled its way back into people's affections, regardless of social class. It's interesting to note, however, that the traditional block printing method has once again become popular, but only within a niche of people who are willing to pay for, and appreciate, the tactility and textural charm that comes with paint printed on paper. Artisans' skills cost – whether it's carving the wood block design or printing the papers accurately – and hand-blocked wallpapers now rank as one of the signifiers of high-end interiors. Few manufacturers still make hand-blocked papers, but for those who do, such as Watts of Westminster and Dunford Wood, there is proving to be a dedicated and discerning market for one of the oldest methods of printing.

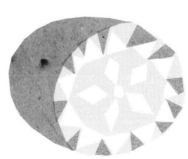

LINOPRINTING

Linoleum was developed as a floor covering in the second half of the 1800s, but it didn't take long for artists and crafters to look beyond its workaday purpose. A group of German expressionists, known as Die Brücke (The Bridge), had been experimenting with traditional woodcuts but soon saw the potential of lino as an alternative – firm enough to print from, soft enough to carve with a sharp chisel, and readily and cheaply available. It also has the added benefit, unlike wood, that it doesn't have a grain, so can be cut in all directions.

The material's accessibility has been one of the reasons for its continued success amongst artists and craftspeople, but there's also an expressive quality to linocuts that other forms of printing tend to miss. The process of cutting out a design is very involved – you are effectively painting with a small chisel, creating lines of different width, length and texture, tapering off to a distinctive point. And, as the ink is rolled onto the lino and impressed onto one piece of paper at a time, no two prints are ever identical.

As a material, traditional lino is harder to carve than more modern, synthetic versions. Some crafters prefer traditional lino for its ability to produce fine detail, while others like softer, synthetic varieties as they're easier to cut, especially on a curve. Either way, linoprinting proved a hit with famous artists such as Picasso and Matisse, while still remaining one of the best methods to introduce children and newcomers to the craft of printing.

STENCILLING

While one group of early humans were busy printing their hands in France's Chauvet caves (see BLOCK PRINTING, pages 60–63), on the other side of the world, in Sulawesi, Indonesia, people were playing with stencils. Made by placing a hand against a cave wall and blowing paint around it, one of these Indonesian hand stencils has been dated to around 39,900 years old and is now thought to be the oldest stencil known in existence.

Throughout history, stencils have been used as a way of producing a repeated design. It's a quick, efficient process, to create a template through which you can press inks, paints or dyes. You can spray, stipple, push, wipe, roll or rub paint through a stencil – onto any flat surface – making it ideal for everything from printing fabrics to wall decoration, book illustration to lettering. Almost every culture has employed stencilling in one form or another – ancient Egyptians used stencils cut from animal skins, while halfway across the globe, isolated Inuit communities came to do almost exactly the same thing with seal skins on Canada's Baffin Island. Fiji's women would decorate bark cloth panels with geometric designs using stencils made from banana leaves while, in the 8th century, Japan developed its own method for stencilling on fabrics, called Katagami. The Europeans loved stencils too – by the Middle Ages we'd embraced the craft as an effective method for decorating walls, furniture, floors and screens, especially in churches.

More recently, stencilling has led a double-life, both a favourite of 1980s interior decorators, who loved its rustic charms, and a technique perfected by graffiti artists. Its ease of use and ability for speedy replication makes it the perfect method for street artists, who need to throw up art quickly and without detection. Who'd have thought Laura Ashley and Banksy had so much in common?

SCREENPRINTING

A close-cousin of STENCILLING (pages 66–67), screenprinting uses a screen made from thin fabric (usually silk or synthetic) stretched tightly over a frame. Just like a stencil, the areas you don't want to print are blocked out, while ink or paint is pushed through the fabric onto the surface below, using a rubber tool known as a squeegee. STENCILLING and screenprinting share so many techniques that it's near impossible to say when one developed into the other; however, what we do know is that, in 1907, an enterprising Englishman, Samuel Simon, patented a design for a screen based on a Japanese model of silk he'd seen.

Just a few years later, the American John Pilsworth patented another version, which could print more than one colour, and commercial screenprinting took off. A technique that works brilliantly with bold blocks of colour, screenprinting became popular with manufacturers of fabrics, wallpapers, posters and advertising material. Some of the most exciting examples of the craft came during the 1930s, when fabric manufacturers worked in collaboration with leading designers of the day – such as Marion Dorn, Ruth Reeves and Dora Batty – to produce brave, new printed textiles in graphic patterns and robust colours.

Pop artists of the 1950s and 60s also loved the commercial, young 'look' of screenprinting – Andy Warhol's Campbell's Soup Cans (1962) – consisting of 32 screenprints – remain the most iconic of them all.

||||||||||||||||||||||||||||||||||||||||||||||||||||||||||||||

DID YOU KNOW?

The word 'squeegee' was first recorded
in the mid 1800s. The squeegee was a
nautical tool, for cleaning, and may have
come from the earlier word 'squeege'
meaning 'to press.'

||||||||||||||||||||||||||||||||||||||||||||||||||||||||||||||

LETTERPRESS

Imagine you were medieval publisher. You wanted to make 50 copies of the same book but your options were limited. You could copy each one out, painstakingly, by hand (see CALLIGRAPHY, pages 56–59) or carve each individual page, into a wooden block, and then print it off (BLOCK PRINTING, pages 60–63). Either way, it was going to be laborious and expensive.

What if you could have a system where you had lots of individual letters and bits of punctuation? You could arrange these pieces of type into words, sentences and paragraphs, lock them into a frame, cover them in ink and press paper against the type to get an impression. Not only would it mean you could print off endless copies of the same page, but you could easily rearrange the individual characters and create something new.

This system – called 'moveable type printing' – was first invented by the Chinese around A.D. 1000, using porcelain type. The Koreans also developed a similar system, using metal type, 200 years later. Amazingly, it didn't catch on, probably due to the fact that both languages had too many individual characters to turn into type.

Fast forward to the middle of the 1400s. Johannes Gutenberg was a German goldsmith and inventor and the first European to use moveable type. But his system was better than any predecessors. Not only did he invent a process for mass-producing movable type, but he also invented better quality, oil-based inks, and the use of a wooden printing press. It was a dynamite combination. Printing suddenly became faster and cheaper, revolutionising access to books and the written word across the Western world.

The Gutenberg press, with its moveable type, remained the standard method of printing text until the 19th century, and continued to be used for books well into the 1970s, by which time it had become commonly known as 'letterpress' printing. While newer, cheaper forms of printing – such as off-set printing and, more recently, digital printing – replaced most of the work done by a letterpress printer, the craft didn't entirely die out, and in recent years has enjoyed a welcome revival.

Its continued popularity is probably down to two factors: first, letterpress requires a level of craftsmanship that appeals to fans of all things handmade. Every step of the process requires detailed care – from lining up the type to operating the presses. For all its mechanisation, letterpress printing relies very much on the talents of the printer to get a sharp, neat imprint. There's also a great deal of artistry in the choices of typeface, the positioning of the elements and the handling of inks and colour.

Second, is the print itself. Letterpress work has a gorgeous tactile quality – each print is subtly different. From the weight of the paper (often handmade) to the gentle indentations made by the metal type, the work feels crafted rather than mass-produced, lending itself to high-end stationery and art prints. The traditional way of letterpress printing is, however, labour intensive. Many artisan printers do still use the original metal moveable type but a new wave of digital letterpressers has emerged, who turn computer images into chemically-etched photopolymer plates to produce intricate, crisp designs.

DID YOU KNOW?

The phrase 'to make a good impression'
comes from letterpress – the job of the
printer was always to get as sharp and
crisp an impression or imprint as possible.

||||||||||||||||||||||||||||||||||||||||||||||||||||||||||||||||||||

CRAFT INVENTIONS

SCISSORS

While Victorian archaeologists were rooting around in a dusty Egyptian tomb they discovered a woman's sewing basket. In it were needles, pins, combs and the most dazzling bronze scissors they'd ever seen. This early pair, dated to the 3rd century B.C., looked like sheep shears, with a bow spring back and thin blades that slid across each other when squeezed together. In fact, this form of shears would have been well established when our Egyptian seamstress was using them. The Greeks, Romans and Egyptians all used similar tools to clip wool, cut hair, snip fabric and trim hedges (the Romans were crazy about topiary).

The origin of 'true' scissors – also known as pivot scissors because they join in the middle – is slightly less clear. Romans made pivoted tongs and other grabbing tools but we can't say for certain that they made pivot scissors, as none have ever been found. The written evidence doesn't help either. The Roman word for scissors, pincers and shears is the same – *forfex* – so we can't tell which type of cutting tool early scribes are talking about.

Skip forward a thousand years, however, and Viking blacksmiths had mastered the art of scissor-making. Sometimes found in female graves, pivot scissors would probably have been part of the essential 'kit' that women carried around at all times, along with a knife, needles and a whetstone (the Viking woman's equivalent of wet wipes, car keys and emergency lip balm). It wasn't until 1760 that scissors were mass manufactured, thanks to William Whiteley & Sons of Sheffield. The same family still make scissors today.

GLUE

Imagine you were a Neanderthal. You want to make a stone weapon, but you need to find a way to attach the handle. The answer? Stick it on. Archaeologists in Italy discovered that early hominids may have been making tar-like glue as far back as 200,000 years ago, by baking rolls of birch bark in the ashes of a fire. The resulting glue would have then been used for hafting, the process of fixing a handle to a piece of stone or bone. Similar discoveries have been made elsewhere, in other isolated regions. Adhesive has been found on stone tools from Sibudu Cave in South Africa, while traces of bitumen have turned up on 40,000-year-old stone tools in Syria.

NEEDLE

A recent excavation in Siberia found the oldest complete needle in the world. It's about 7.5cm long, delicately carved from bird bone (complete with an eye for thread), and dates to an astonishing 50,000 years old. What's even more incredible is that archaeologists don't think it was made by modern humans but rather by a long extinct species of early humans called Denisovans, a close relative of Neanderthals. The implications are extraordinary. Not only was this ancient subspecies sewing clothing, blankets and perhaps even shoes, but they had the technology and tools to make the needle in the first place.

PENCIL

In Ancient Rome, if you wanted to write you'd use a stylus. Made from lead, these metal sticks would leave a mark on a sheet of papyrus or a wax tablet. Pencils, as we know them, started with the discovery of a huge deposit of graphite in the Lake District in the 1560s. Local farmers noticed that the graphite (which they wrongly named 'black lead') was useful for marking sheep; it left a lovely dark smudge but was brittle to handle, so the graphite needed some kind of protective outer layer. People used string, paper or sheepskin initially but it wasn't long before an Italian couple, the Bernacottis, invented a method for hollowing out a wooden stick into which you slipped a thin strip of graphite. These early pencils were flat, like carpenter's pencils. The oldest pencil in existence was found in the rafters of a 17th-century German house. Historians believe the carpenter left it there by mistake, where it had remained unnoticed for 300 years. Curiously, the word 'pencil' comes from the Latin *penicullus*, or 'little tail' and described an artist's brush. (The word 'penis' also comes from the same Latin word.)

CRAYON

At the site of an ancient lake in North Yorkshire, England, archaeologists found the world's oldest crayon (see THATCHING, pages 170–173 and WOODWORKING, pages 174–177). The small object, made from red ochre, belonged to a Stone Age tribe who lived 10,000 years ago, at a site now known as Star Carr, and may have been used to colour animal skins or draw on rocks.

RULER

If you want to measure the length of something you need to have a standardised system that everyone agrees on. Today we use centimetres and metres, for example, but the earliest distance unit was the cubit. A cubit, the length between a man's elbow and his middle finger, was used to measure everything from timber to travel distances. Even Noah's Ark was described in cubits.

But this presents one small problem, everyone's arms are slightly different lengths. Many cultures developed 'official cubits' to solve this problem; stone, wooden or metal rulers kept by officials against which citizens could calibrate their own measurements. The oldest cubit ruler dates to around 2600 B.C. and was discovered in Nippur, now modern-day Iraq. Another ruler – calibrated with spectacular accuracy – was found in Mohenjo-daro, Pakistan, and dates to a similar time (2400 B.C.). In Egypt, just to confuse things, they had two cubit measurements – the short cubit (about 45cm) and the long cubit (about 52cm). The short cubit was used to measure monuments, and was the same unit of measurement used by the Romans, Greeks and Hebrews. The long cubit was for everyday use. For longer distances, Egyptian surveyors marked out a rope (see ROPEMAKING, pages 104–105) into lengths of 100 cubits (about 50m) to create an early form of the modern measuring tape. The word 'cubit' comes from the Latin *cubitus* or 'elbow' and the ancient craft of hedgelaying still measures in cubits today.

TEXTILES, CLOTH & LEATHER

FUR & LEATHER

The story of textiles is really the story of nudity. At some point, we must have decided that skipping around naked wasn't practical and reached for the nearest bearskin. But what does the evidence tell us? Fabrics don't survive long in the archaeological record – rotting away or crumbling to dust in just a few years – but there are a few tiny clues textile historians can hang their theories on.

The first clue, amazingly, comes not from any great discovery of a haul of textiles, but rather from the fact that scientists recently found out body lice – which can only survive in clothing – evolved about 170,000 years ago. While it's a disgusting thought, it's helpful to know that where there are lice, there must be people wearing garments.

The second clue comes when you analyse just how cold the environment would have been for our ancestors. Archaeologists argue over the precise dates, but it seems that modern humans evolved in Africa and then migrated to the rest of the world, in waves, possibly starting as early as 200,000 years ago. Clothing would have allowed them to cope with a variety of cooler, wetter environments, not just the balmy African savannah. Your birthday suit just isn't going to cut it in the Siberian tundra.

But here's an interesting point. Modern humans weren't the first early humans to leave Africa. It's thought that around 500,000 years ago a very early group of archaic humans left Africa. Gradually these archaic humans split into two groups: the Denisovans, who spread into the east, and the Neanderthals, who occupied Europe and the west. Studies have shown that these early migrants wouldn't have been able to survive outside Africa without a substantial amount of clothing, especially during the winter months, and would have had to cover up at least 80 per cent of their bodies, especially the extremities such as hands and feet. Ergo, modern humans didn't invent clothes. Quite how sophisticated the archaic human's garments would have been is a moot point; were Neanderthals sewing clothes together or just wrapping hides around themselves, for example? Again, all we can do is make deductions from the tiny clues left behind.

The earliest clothes were made from animal skins. A stone tool site in Germany reveals that Neanderthals were probably processing leather as long ago as 100,000 years. Other excavations, in southwest France, found Neanderthal bone tools – called 'lissoirs' – which are used for smoothing animal skins. These date from around 50,000 years ago and demonstrate that Neanderthals were working leather in a sophisticated way, making it smooth and waterproof.

What was missing from this picture, however, was any kind of evidence that these animal skins were sewn together to create tailored clothes. Instead, it was assumed that Neanderthals used awls to punch holes in the leather, which were then crudely laced together using strips of sinew or other natural cordage. This kind of craftwork produces loose tunics and cloaks, but not the kind of close-fitting clothing that we find modern humans creating much later.

In fact, Neanderthal man's inability to make decent clothes was often cited as one of the likely reasons he became extinct. When temperatures plummeted in the last Ice Age, modern man, with his snug-fitting, fur-lined, hooded coat (think Stone Age parka), managed to ride out the storm. Poor old Neanderthal man, it was thought, struggled to cope in his ill-fitting bearskins and draughty cape.

Then, as always happens with archaeology, something turned up that muddied this picture. A sewing needle appeared in a cave in Siberia (see CRAFT INVENTIONS, pages 74-75). It was 50,000 years old, beautifully crafted, and belonged to a

(Neanderthal's eastern cousin). The presence of this one needle has cast doubt on the notion that only modern man had the intelligence and skill to get stitching. Perhaps, just perhaps, the craft is even older than we ever imagined.

Whatever the truth surrounding its origins, modern humans took leather craft and sewing to a whole new level of artistry and sophistication. Since the 1991 discovery of Ötzi the Iceman in a European glacier, scientists have gleaned a wealth of information from his 5,300-year-old mummified remains, not least just how important leather clothes were to our ancestors' day-to-day survival. Ötzi was found with a full outfit of preserved clothing, including a long coat, skin leggings, fur hat and grass-stuffed shoes – one of the oldest pair of shoes ever found (see THE HISTORY OF CRAFTED CLOTHING, pages 120–121).

Research into how these clothes were created reveals that Ötzi tailored his clothes with skins taken from domesticated sheep, goats and cattle, as well as hides from wild brown bears and roe deer. His leather shoes were so comfortable and well-suited to his chilly environment that a modern shoe company, OTZ Shoes, now makes walkers' footwear based on Ötzi's original design.

SPINNING & WEAVING

One of the interesting facts about Ötzi and his wardrobe is that, despite his glorious ensemble of leather and fur, not a shred of wool or woven clothing was found. He did, however, have a woven grass mat.

We often think of woven fabrics, such as wool, linen and cotton, as soft. But a huge variety of materials can be woven together, from grasses to strips of tree bark, to create everything from fishing nets to cloth, baskets to floor coverings. While these perishable objects rarely survive, we can look at the tools associated with weaving, such as loom weights or spindle whorls, or traces of weaving patterns that have been imprinted onto a soft surface, such as clay, often by accident. Experts also examine human statues and figurines from antiquity to gain valuable clues about the kinds of fabrics and clothing that would have been worn thousands of years ago.

Until recently, it was thought that weaving had been invented by farming communities between 10,000 and 5,000 years ago. The theory being that, when a community is settled and producing more food than it needs, it can support people who are engaged in activities other than growing produce. In other words, hunting and gathering is so utterly time-consuming as

a way of life, there's neither the time nor the resources for anyone to sit down and play around with fabrics or knit a Christmas jumper.

Recent discoveries are challenging that idea. A large collection of clay fragments found in the Czech Republic was carefully scrutinised for patterns; archaeologists found something surprising. Many of the pieces of clay had impressions of woven fibres pressed into them. What's more, the impressions indicated an astonishing variety of weaving techniques. Whoever these clay fragments belonged to knew how to do a number of things, including open twining (making baskets or nets that have large spaces between the threads), closed twining (making tightly woven baskets for carrying grain or liquids) and plain weaving. Twining can done by hand but, critically, plain weaving needs a loom. And the age of these clay fragments? About 27,000 years old.

So, if Stone Age hunter-gatherers were weaving, what were they making? Experts involved in the analysis of the clay fragments (and subsequent studies of other finds) think that these early societies were probably using weaving techniques to create a multitude of everyday and ritual objects, from bags to hats, caps, baskets, sashes, skirts, necklaces, belts and nets for catching small prey, such as hares.

If early societies had the know-how, why didn't they weave all their clothing? And why didn't woven textiles become the norm until almost 20,000 years later? The answer is that, just because a technology exists, it's only useful if people need it. Central Europe would have been a cold place 27,000 years ago, still in the grip of the last Ice Age. Animal skins and fur would have offered far greater protection against the cold than woven fabrics ever could. Woven cloth couldn't compete with furs and skins until the world warmed up, starting around 11,000 years ago, and even then, plain weaving was a technology best suited to warmer climates and more settled populations. Perhaps this explains why, even as late as 5300 years ago, the only woven item our European friend Ötzi carried was a mat, made from alpine swamp grass.

As with many crafts, it seems that several isolated cultures figured out how to weave simultaneously but independently. Scraps of woven fabric – all dated to a roughly similar period – have turned up in places as far apart as South America and Turkey,

Switzerland and Asia. One of the most poignant pieces of fabric ever discovered was in the ancient city of Çatalhöyük, now modern-day Turkey. There, archaeologists found a 9000-year-old piece of woven hemp linen – the oldest example ever found – carefully wrapped around the body of a baby, in the grounds of a burned-out house.

The process of weaving breaks down into two neat stages. The first is the creation of the yarn or thread. This is done by twisting separate fibres of wool, cotton or hair into one stronger, longer thread that can then be woven into cloth (or KNITTED, CROCHETED etc).

To twist the separate fibres, one of the oldest methods is to use a 'drop spindle'. It's a brilliantly simple but effective tool that uses a combination of gravity and its spinning motion to twist lengths of fibres into yarn or thread. At the base of the spindle is a small circular weight – called a 'spindle whorl' – which helps keep the fibres taut while they are being spun, and adds momentum to the spin. Drop spindles were often highly decorated and turn up in numerous quantities at excavations around the world, fashioned from everything from stone to ceramic, bone, wood and lead. Their presence in large numbers, both in excavations of villages and towns and in remote areas away from settlements, suggests that people (probably women and young girls) carried their spinning

equipment with them at all times, so they could squeeze in a few minutes of valuable spinning whenever a spare moment arose between work or childcare. By the 15th century, the spinning wheel had replaced the drop spindle in Europe, only to be supplanted by industrial-scale machines such as the 'spinning jenny' and 'spinning mule' at the beginning of the Industrial Revolution.

For all its uniformity, machine-spun yarn often lacks the character and individual quirks of hand-spun fibres. Many weavers still prefer to use these distinctive 'lumpy' yarns created on a drop spindle or spinning wheel, while spinning as a craft in itself has enjoyed a gentle resurgence, especially amongst people interested in KNITTING and CROCHET, and makers who want to support local wool production and rare breed livestock.

The second stage of weaving involves taking two sets of yarn or thread and criss-crossing them to create a textile. The threads running lengthways are known as the 'warp' and are fixed in place, either stretched tightly over a frame or pinned onto a flat surface. The threads that run from side to side – known as the 'weft' – pass over and under these warp threads to create a woven pattern.

Over the centuries weavers have come up with different ways to hold the warp threads under tension and weave the weft thread over and under. Initially, this may have been done by pegging or weighting the warp threads to the ground but it wasn't long before crafters came up with a specialised frame; the warp-weighted loom – where the warp hangs down vertically and is keep taut with stone weights – has been around for at least 6000 years while the thousand-year-old treadle handloom – a machine where the weaver presses pedals to lift the warp while simultaneously throwing the shuttle carrying the weft yarn – is still used in the production of artisan fabrics today.

While most modern fabric is machine-woven on an industrial scale, it's worth noting that an increasing number of designers and makers are reviving hand-weaving skills as a way to create unique, one-off pieces. As with many crafts, hand weaving gives rise to an end product that's full of subtle irregularities. Buyers also love the idea that a fabric has a distinct provenance, heritage and back-story.

Contemporary crafters are reinventing weaving, creating new fabrics and textile art that are both fresh and deeply grounded in traditional techniques; many of these practitioners – Maryanne Moodie and Victoria Manganiello, for example – exploit the tactile quality of weaving, incorporate unusual threads, and play around with the rhythm and mathematical rules of the weaving process. Wall hangings and smaller pieces of textile art have also proved

a particularly popular strand for the modern weaver, with contemporary crafters such as Judit Just and Laura Strutt creating dazzling woven panels, often combining neons, neutrals and pastels. It's an accessible craft, not only with its Instagrammable images, but also the tools and skills of the trade are relatively straightforward – novices soon find they can pick up the basics, such as changing colours or adding texture with different fibres. The appeal for many isn't just the finished article, however. As with many crafts, the meditative, absorbing nature of the process is just as enjoyable, and important, as the end result.

DYEING

Wool and other natural fibres have a limited palette of browns and off-whites, so it must have been a beige world until people started playing with dyes. Thankfully, the natural world provides a wealth of hues – from colourful plants to pigments in clay – and it doesn't take long for dyed textiles to appear in the archaeological record.

A team of palaeobiologists recently stumbled upon flax fibres that are astonishingly ancient, dating back more than 34,000 years. The fibres, which turned up in a cave in the Republic of Georgia, are not only the oldest ever found but also the first dyed fibres to be discovered, including threads that were dyed black, grey, turquoise and pink.

Over on the other side of the world, a 6,000-year-old scrap of blue striped fabric – not dissimilar to modern-day 'pyjama-stripe' ticking – was uncovered on the north coast of Peru, while Tutankhamun's tomb and the ruins of Pompeii both revealed examples of dyed red cloth.

But where did prehistoric people get their colours from? Natural dyes are derived from three sources: plants, minerals and insects. In Europe people experimented with plant dyes extracted from woad (blue), weld (yellow) and madder (red), while cultures in warmer climates also made use of indigo (blue), logwood (violets and greys) and brazilwood (red). Other sources of dyes included the kermes and cochineal bugs (both red), shellfish (purples and blues) and mineral compounds such as iron oxide (reds and browns).

It's a testament to the effectiveness of natural dyes that they continued to be used exclusively until the 1850s. In 1856, however, during an Easter break from college, 18-year-old chemistry student, William Henry Perkin, decided to experiment with a cure for malaria. The experiment failed, but instead Perkin accidentally created a vivid purple colour – the first synthetic dye ever created. Since then, synthetic dyes have opened up a world of vivid, rich, colour-fast pigments to both manufacturers and crafters.

However, the story of natural dyes didn't end with Perkin. The Arts and Crafts movement of the early 20th century revived nostalgia for traditional dyeing techniques and plant-based colours, while during both World Wars nettles were used to dye uniforms thanks to trade embargoes and shortages of synthetic pigments.

Over the last twenty years, there's been a renewed interest in sustainable fabrics and dyes. The majority of textile dyeing takes place in developing countries, where health and safety legislation and environmental regulations are often flouted. Textile dyeing and treatment is also the second largest polluter in the world, beaten only by agriculture. Natural dyes have once again come to the fore and, although perhaps not suited to large-scale production, can be grown sustainably and at a smaller, artisanal level. Craft pioneers such as US-based Audrey Louise Reynolds, a self-taught artisanal fabric dyer, are also helping to ensure that the future for natural dyes, once again, looks bright.

||||||||||||||||||||||||||||||||||||||||||||||||||||||||||||||||||||

DID YOU KNOW?

Most natural dyes need a fixative or 'mordant' to stop the colour from bleeding out of the fabric when it's washed or worn. The word *mordant* comes from the French *mordre*, 'to bite', the idea being that the colour 'bites' into the fabric.

||||||||||||||||||||||||||||||||||||||||||||||||||||||||||||||||||||

WET FELTING

If you've ever had to brush furballs from a cat, you'll know just how tough matted hair can be. Felting works on the same principle; you take a handful of hair or fur fibres and use heat, moisture and pressure to mat them together. It's a straightforward process, but a brilliantly effective one. It's also a fabric-making process with a number of added benefits: you don't need a loom, the resulting fabric doesn't fray because the fibres aren't in any particular orientation, plus it's hardwearing and can hold its shape. No wonder felt has been a favourite fabric for thousands of years.

There are some fantastic myths that tell the story of the first felters. One legend recounts the tale of St. Clement and St. Christopher who, fleeing persecution from the Romans, wrapped their feet in wool to prevent blisters and – through a combination of foot perspiration and pressure – accidentally created felt inside their shoes. Another talks of a Persian shepherd who, stamping in frustration because he didn't have a loom, trampled his fleece into felt. The best narrative, however, comes from Noah's Ark. The story goes that, as the animals went in two by two, they shed their hairs on the floor of the ark. Such was the frantic trampling that, when Noah looked down, the hairs had turned into a carpet of felt.

Intuitively, it feels safe to assume that people learned how to felt before they could WEAVE (pages 82–85) – the technology and raw materials are, after all, simpler to produce than the spun yarn and loom needed for woven fabrics – and yet there are no examples of felt that pre-date the earliest woven fabrics. This is, however, more likely a reflection of just how few fabrics withstand the test of time, rather than an indication of which fabric came first.

What we do know, however, is that thanks to some miraculous archaeological discoveries, ancient cultures used felt for almost every purpose imaginable. One such discovery was the Pazyryk Iron Age burial tombs, in the Altai Mountains of Siberia (see DÉCOUPAGE, pages 46–47). The Pazyryk people were wealthy horse-riding nomads; their tombs were elaborate and stuffed to the brim with textiles, furniture and other household goods. Normally these wouldn't have survived the centuries but, thanks to the frozen conditions of the mountains, rare examples of APPLIQUÉ felt wall hangings, rugs and other objects have been preserved.

The most famous of these burial tombs belonged to a wealthy young woman, nicknamed the Altai Lady. Not only was she buried with six horses, that were sacrificed to accompany her in the afterlife, but her wooden coffin was decorated with leather APPLIQUÉ figures of deer and snow leopards. When discovered, the Altai Lady was laid on thick, soft felt and was wearing, amongst other rich textiles, thigh-length felt leggings and a metre high felt headdress. Other nearby tombs gave up similar felt treasures, including felt saddles, felt hats, felt APPLIQUÉ panels and a magnificent white felt swan stuffed with reindeer wool.

Whether the nomads of the Altai region were the first felters is impossible to say, but what we do know is that they were absolute masters of the craft. Using local sheep wool, the Pazyryk created many different types of felt; some fine and malleable felt for clothing, wall hangings and headgear, and other coarser and thicker felt for saddle clothes and horse masks. We also know that the skills for felt making passed from nomadic tribes to the Chinese. We first see mentions of felt in Chinese records towards the end of the Zhou Dynasty (around the 4th to 3rd century B.C.), not as clothing, but as felt mattresses to sleep on. Interestingly, Siberian nomads still cover their traditional tent-like homes – yurts – with felt today.

NEEDLE FELTING

If you spend any time browsing crafters on Etsy or watching craft tutorials, you can't have missed the emergence of needle felting. It's a method of dry felting that requires very little beyond a handful of wool fibres, a felting needle and a forgiving surface. The process is simple: you repeatedly stab or poke the wool fibres with the needle. The needle used is slightly barbed and, every time it comes into contact with the wool, the barbs agitate the fibres in the wool to cause them to 'stick' together. For anyone new to craft, needle felting is a satisfying and quick entry point into 2D embellishments and 3D sculpting with wool. It makes a popular choice for kids and adult workshops as it requires little training and even fewer tools. That said, in the right hands, needle felting can produce extraordinary results – more akin to sculpture than textile crafts. Pioneers such as US fibre artist Stephanie Metz, for example, take felt in an unexpected direction, creating pieces that explore anatomy, the human form and animal biology in often startling and bizarre ways.

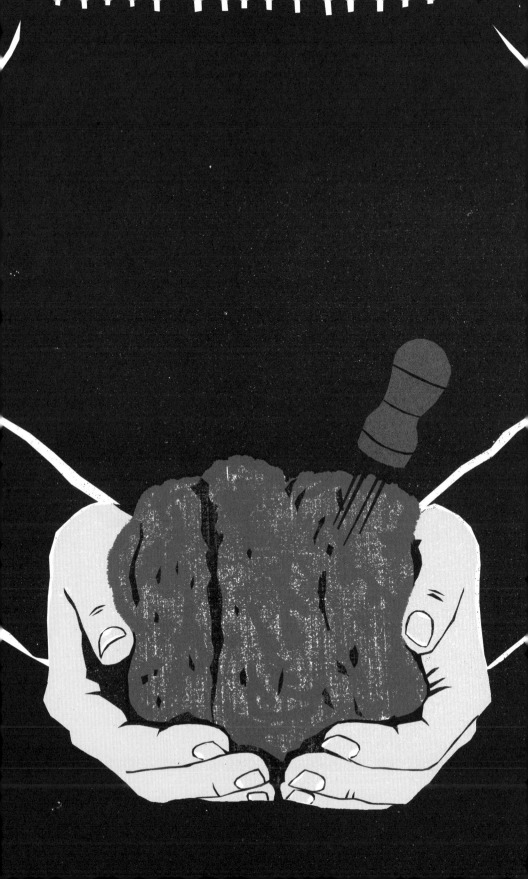

APPLIQUÉ

In 1323 B.C., when the Egyptian pharaoh Tutankhamun died at the tender age of 18, he was buried with enough clothes to last him in the afterlife, including piles of loincloths, tunics, kilts, shawls, socks and gloves. Just like a modern wardrobe, while some of these clothes were plain and everyday, a selection were gorgeously elaborate and decorated. Among the clothes and other textiles were a number of items that had been painstakingly appliquéd, including a faux leopard skin with appliqué spots, a pair of wings appliquéd with a falcon and vultures, and a child's tunic with an appliqué collar.

Appliqué is a technique that involves stitching smaller cut-outs onto a larger foundation cloth. The term 'appliqué' comes from the French appliquer, 'to apply' or 'to put on', and it's tempting to think that appliqué must have developed as a technique for patching up old clothes. From the finds at Tutankhamun's tomb, however, and subsequent discoveries, including appliqué wall hangings in Siberian tombs (see WET FELTING, pages 90-91) and appliquéd mummified animal wrappings from Saqqara, Egypt, it would seem that appliqué has more often been a craft not of necessity, but of pomp and ceremony. During the Middle Ages, for

example, elaborate appliqué was often used to decorate heraldic banners and ecclesiastical textiles.

In fact, it's interesting to note that throughout the world appliqué is still used by many cultures to embellish ceremonial and ritually significant pieces, from the 'mola' appliqué clothing of the Kuna women in Panama to the traditional textiles of the Hmong hill tribes of southeast Asia. In Africa, the appliqué raffia textiles of the Kuba, in the Democratic Republic of Congo, reflect the shared religious beliefs of the group, while the Fon of Benin use appliqué cloth as a way to record a deceased person's merits and friendship. Appliqué is also a popular technique in QUILTING (pages 100-101), where scraps of fabric are turned into folk art full of symbolism relating to family, history and community.

SEWING
& EMBROIDERY

With the sewing needle, came the stitch. It's difficult to imagine just how old sewing really is (see CRAFT INVENTIONS, pages 74-75), but with the knowledge that the earliest needle found so far is 50,000 years old, it's safe to assume we've been stitching for a very long time indeed.

At first, our attempts would have been crude and irregular. But practice makes perfect and soon not only would stitching have served a clear, practical goal but it would have also become a means to express creativity and skill. That's when sewing becomes embroidery – the point at which the stitch is a decorative embellishment, rather than solely a means of structural fixing.

With its wealth of fabulous fabrics and clothing, Tutankhamun's tomb divulged a whole host of early examples of embroidery and APPLIQUÉ (pages 94-95), crafted by skilled artisans in the pharaoh's palace. What's remarkable from these finds is that, even as early as thirteen hundred years before the birth of Christ, crafters had already mastered a range of stitches recognisable to modern embroiderers, including chain, twisted chain, dot, running, stem, satin and coral stitch. Other early

examples of embroidery pop up all over the globe, from a 4th century B.C. chain-stitched silk garment found at Mashan, China to fragments of a cloak used to wrap mummified bodies in Peru, over 2000 years ago.

The subject matter and patterns of historical embroideries may differ, but they share common truths: that embroidery was skilled, time-consuming and, therefore, expensive. Embroidery was not only an expression of ideas and artistic sensibilities, but also a status symbol, a signifier of wealth and power. Nowhere was this truer than medieval England and its *opus anglicanum*.

Imagine a world where most people cannot read. If you want to tell the story of Christ in this world, it would be best done through pictures. In medieval England few things would have been more impressive than a church filled with vibrant embroideries, altar hangings and vestments resplendent with Biblical tales and gruesome martyrdoms. The phrase *opus anglicanum* translates to 'English work' and describes these dazzling embroideries. Some were created by nuns and noblewomen, but such was the demand for large and numerous pieces that special workshops were established by merchants and patrons in London, employing both men and women to produce embroideries of staggering intricacy and design.

Between the 12th and 14th centuries, England could barely keep up with orders for its exquisite needlework from diplomats, courtiers and kings. Rome was especially smitten; for successive popes, the *opus anglicanum* struck the perfect balance of visible splendour and pious subject matter. In fact, most of the work that survives from this period was designed for use in church, from clothing to shrine covers, robes to altar hangings.

We do know, however, that medieval clients also asked for other, more worldly items – book covers, wall hangings and slippers, for example – beautifully embroidered with gold, silk and silver threads, pearls and jewels. Whether ecclesiastical or secular, English embroidery became a status symbol and popular diplomatic gift. In 1317, Queen Isabella, wife of Edward III, was thought to have paid the equivalent of £40,000 for an embroidered cloak to give to her bishop.

In the modern world, the enforced slowness and depth of concentration needed to practise embroidery has, perhaps, put off a younger generation of potential crafters. And yet, these are the very things about embroidery that make it such an important creative form. Embroidery has always been a craft that demands precision and care, alongside artistic expression, and it's this combination that makes it a particularly calming and fulfilling craft. The Royal School of Needlework – an international centre of excellence – knows this only too well and has, among other programmes, devised ways of reaching out to new, young audiences. Their 'Stitch a Selfie' project, for example, encouraged older, school-age girls and boys to create embroidered pictures of themselves that focused less on technical ability and more on imagination and self-expression through stitching. Equally, the work of polymath Kaffe Fassett – who not only designs and paints but also sews, quilts and knits – also shows that embroidery can be more about 'painting with thread' than worrying about painstaking detail.

||||||||||||||||||||||||||||||||||||||||||||||||||||||||||||||||||||

DID YOU KNOW?

'Embroider', 'braid' and 'braddle' may all be related words, from the centuries old Middle English word *brad* or *brod* meaning spike, needle or prick.

||||||||||||||||||||||||||||||||||||||||||||||||||||||||||||||||||||

QUILTING

At the turn of the last century, archaeologists found a tiny little ivory statue of a pharaoh in the Tomb of Osiris, Egypt. This diminutive relic – which stands little more than 8cm high – gives us the first big clue about the origins of quilting. The figure depicts a king wearing a heavy cloak. Such is the detail in the carving that textile historians believe they can make out the diamond patterns of a quilted fabric. If it's true, that puts the earliest evidence of quilting as far back as 3000 B.C. But Egypt wasn't the only kingdom with a passion for patchwork. Excavations in south central China uncovered the tomb of a rich woman who was buried with a selection of superb silk garments and fabrics, including quilted jackets, quilted shoes and a luxurious quilted bedspread, all dating back to sometime between 771–221 B.C. Other early finds – from a Siberian quilted rug (1st century B.C.) to a plush Uzbekistan slipper (circa 8th century A.D.) – all point to a quilting tradition that starts in North Africa and Asia, before spreading to the rest of the world.

It's surprising that quilting, which is now strongly associated with women and female community, became popular in Europe thanks to the bloodthirsty Crusades. The soldiers, who were returning from fighting in the Muslim Empire, brought back a selection of quilted underclothes. Whilst out in the Middle East, they'd discovered that not only did the local quilted textiles offer extra comfort against the weather, but also made their armour more bearable and offered an extra level of protection against arrows and other weapons. In some instances, lower ranks had to rely solely on quilted clothes; chain-mail and armour being too expensive for the ordinary man.

It's worth mentioning that quilted items may have occasionally been seen in Europe at an early date, but quite how they got there we don't know. One recent example came from an excavation of a 5th-century burial site in Germany; there, a quilted textile was found draped over the entire length of a woman's body. Whether the quilt was imported, shipped in from the eastern Mediterranean or western Asia, or made locally remains unknown.

The medieval European elite, however, loved the new fashion for quilting and exploited the craft to its full potential. From bedspreads to wall hangings, baby bonnets to petticoats, the insulating properties of quilts made them the ideal material for life in cold, draughty manor houses and grand homes. A few examples remain from the medieval period; one notable survivor is the 'Tristan Quilt', made in Sicily sometime at the end of the 1300s and now in the Victoria & Albert Museum in London. Experts argue over whether it's a bedspread or a wall hanging, but all agree that the subject matter is a lively interpretation of the legend of Tristan and Isolde, a tragic love story and favourite ripping yarn of the Middle Ages.

From Europe, the craft travelled with colonists to North America during the 17th and 18th centuries, where early settlers established quilting as a popular craft and an opportunity for social cohesion. Large quilts, such as bedspreads, made by groups of women and young girls, were often associated with special occasions or rites of passage, such as marriage or childbirth. The patterns and motifs often embodied the lives and milestones of the women who made them, and were used as a way of expressing ideas that weren't always possible to talk about in the public arena. One particularly remarkable woman was a quilt maker called Harriet Powers. Born a slave in Georgia, in 1837, Harriet used quilting as a way to express her thoughts and ideas when other routes of expression were closed off to her. Harriet's spectacular quilts – of which only two survive – display a blend of Biblical tales, traditional African craft techniques and storytelling.

MODERN QUILTING

In recent years, the modern quilt movement has shifted emphasis towards a clean, pared-down aesthetic. The quilts are no less exciting or visually rich, however, but instead focus on bold designs, new fabrics and abstractions of traditional quilt patterns. Many of these modern quilts include large sections of single colours, improvisation and negative space. They also take traditional quilt blocks or shapes and use them in new, surprising ways – creating textiles that are more like modernist paintings than folksy fabric. Modern quilters have also embraced technology to spread their message. Not only have digital cameras and cutting-edge fabrics added to the tools and materials at their disposal, but social media has provided a welcoming forum for like-minded crafters. The Modern Quilt Guild, for example, was started in 2009 as a way of bringing together a growing online community of modern quilters. Today, the guild has over 10,000 members and more than 160 local guilds across the world.

|||||||||||||||||||||||||||||||||||||||||||||||||||||||||||||||||

DID YOU KNOW?

The word 'quilt' originally comes from *culcita,* **the Latin for a stuffed mattress, filled sack or cushion.**

|||||||||||||||||||||||||||||||||||||||||||||||||||||||||||||||||

ROPEMAKING

Until recently, the earliest evidence we had for making twisted fibres dated back to around 34,000 years ago. The clues came from two places: one was the discovery of dyed flax cord in a cave in Georgia (see DYEING, pages 88–89) and the other was a series of impressions of twisted fibres pressed into clay in the Czech Republic (see WEAVING, pages 82–87).

Both suggested that ancient hunter-gatherers were the first to make thin rope for a multitude of uses – from hafting stone tools to weaving baskets, making nets to sewing animal skins. Then a recent find changed all that; archaeologists working on a site in southeast France uncovered twisted plant fibres – an early attempt at string – that date back 90,000 years. Not only that, it seems that our early ropemakers were, in fact, Neanderthals, who had learned how to make it themselves, rather than copy the technique from modern humans.

Evidence of chunkier rope comes much later, but is no less revealing. Archaeologists had long wondered how prehistoric artists at the famous Lascaux caves in France had managed to access such a difficult site. The chance discovery of a remnant of ancient rope convinced many that our Palaeolithic painters had made and used rope to climb into the caves over 17,000 years ago.

When it comes to making rope on any scale, and with any uniformity, we look to Ancient Egypt. Many of the surviving tombs display wonderfully detailed scenes from ropemaking workshops; one of the earliest dates from 2600 B.C. and shows a man and a boy with the inscription 'Twisting ropes of boat building'. In another scene, the boy is shown passing over two coils of light cordage, saying, 'My father, here is your rope'.

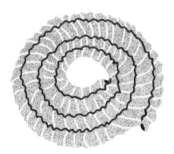

||||||||||||||||||||||||||||||||||||||||||||||||||||||||||||||||

DID YOU KNOW?

Hemp was used for ropemaking for thousands of years. It was often known by its folk name – 'gallows grass' – a bleak reference to rope's darker purpose as a hangman's noose.

||||||||||||||||||||||||||||||||||||||||||||||||||||||||||||||||

Ropemaking was a pivotal craft for the Egyptians, whether for use in shipbuilding, tethering livestock, binding tools or pyramid construction. Ropes were even used by Egyptian surveyors as a tool to measure large distances. The Egyptian phrase for a surveyor was a 'rope stretcher' and surveying was known as 'stretching a rope' (see CRAFT INVENTIONS, pages 74–75).

One of the downsides of ropemaking is that the size of your workspace limits the length of rope it is possible to make, unless you splice together shorter lengths. From the Middle Ages onwards, many of the great European maritime nations needed longer lengths of rope, especially for rigging the taller ships. Rather than splicing rope together – which always creates weak points – a new method was devised, which used 'rope-walks'. Often outside, these long, straight pathways or covered walks could accommodate substantial lengths of rope at one time. Many coastal city streets still bear the name of their ropemaking past. Rope Walks, for example, is an area of long, parallel streets in Liverpool that were once used by ropemakers, a craft that dominated the area until the 19th century. Similarly, Ropemaker Street in London is just one of the many ropewalks that sprung up around the medieval city to service the growing shipping trade. (Incidentally, it's

also the street where author of *Robinson Crusoe*, Daniel Defoe, died, broke, unknown and in hiding from his creditors). Amazingly, a working ropewalk still exists just outside London, at Chatham's naval dockyard; Master Ropemakers still use the $1/4$-mile-long ropewalk on the site that dates back more than 400 years.

MACRAMÉ

Deep in the British Museum sits a carving that dates back to 850 B.C. Looking out from the sculpted stone is an Assyrian warrior dressed, not in cumbersome metal armour, but a rather lovely macramé fringed tunic. It's one of the earliest representations we have of the craft and shows that knotted fabrics have been around for a very long time indeed (the oldest example is actually another 3000 years old, a piece of macramé netting from Ancient Egypt).

Macramé is a craft that, in all probability, grew out of the need to finish off the loose ends of a woven cloth once it was taken off the loom. Knotting the warp and weft threads (see WEAVING, pages 82–87) into a fringe not only made practical sense, but also offered weavers a valuable opportunity to add extra ornamentation to an otherwise simple piece of fabric such as a shawl or towel. Interestingly, the word macramé probably isn't French, as it sounds, but may come from the Turkish *makrama* (meaning towel) and the Arabic *miqrama* (fringed veil), which both derive from an older word *qarama*, meaning to 'nibble at the edges'.

It's not clear how macramé came to Europe, but the Moorish invasion of Spain in the 8th century and the Crusades 300 years later provided plenty of chances for people to see, copy and perfect the craft for their own purposes. Nuns added macramé details to religious clothes and altar cloths, for example, while sailors knotted useful items such as bell pulls, lanyards and belts, selling their work at ports and spreading the craft into far-flung places such as the New World and North America.

Macramé finally made its way onto English shores in the late 1600s. Queen Mary was a fanatical macramé maker, running up huge bills on fine silks, teaching her ladies-in-waiting the craft and, according to one observer, was 'always knotting threads'. Queen Charlotte, wife of the famously 'mad' King George III, was also an avid macramist and the Victorians – always partial to frilly ornamentation – loved its potential, taking every opportunity to add knotted trims to everything from tableclothes to ball gowns.

In recent memory, many people view the 1970s as the decade of macramé, especially in the UK and US. No self-respecting homeowner would be without their macramé plant hanger or knotted wall hanging, and the craze fitted in perfectly with wider ideas about natural, eco-friendly materials and the importance of handmade objects in the home. After a brief lull at the end of the 20th century, macramé is once again cool – it's gentle aesthetic and home-spun appeal striking a chord with millennials – and Instagram crafters such as Emily Katz are bringing their own, laid-back and stylish version of macramé to a brand new, eager audience.

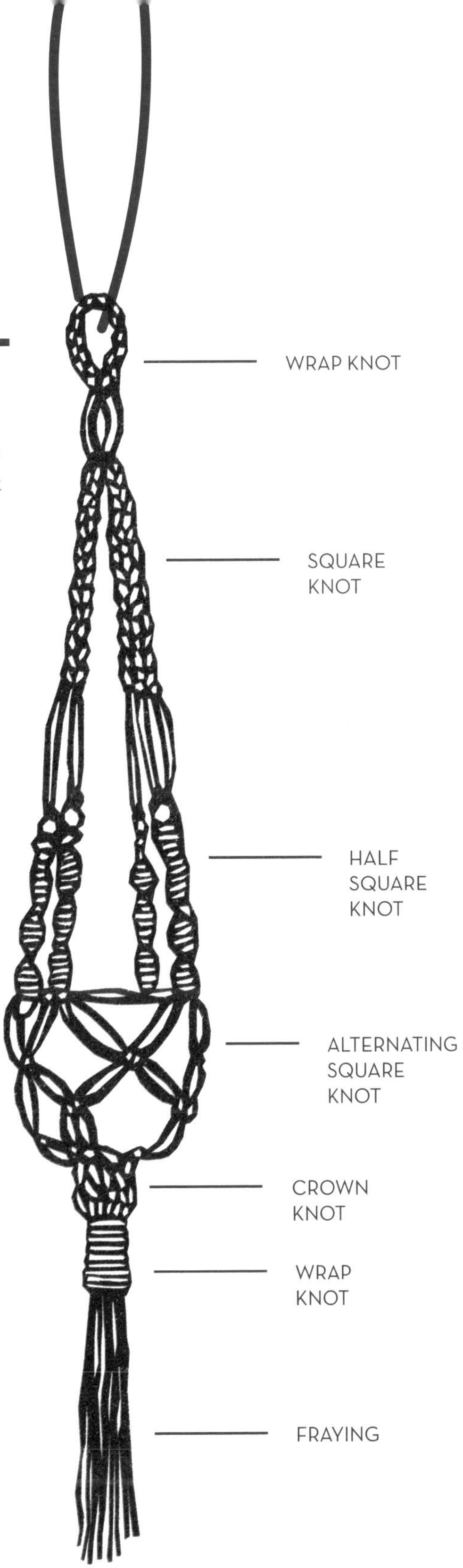

WRAP KNOT

SQUARE KNOT

HALF SQUARE KNOT

ALTERNATING SQUARE KNOT

CROWN KNOT

WRAP KNOT

FRAYING

KNITTING, NÅLEBINDING & CROCHET

It's clear we've been messing about with string and yarn for tens of thousands of years (see ROPEMAKING, pages 104–105, and DYEING, pages 88–89). The urge to experiment, and test a material's properties, is just one of the brilliant things about being human. Considering our insatiable appetite for fiddling with stuff, it's not difficult to imagine that somewhere, while idly twisting plant fibres, someone decided to see what would happen when the fibres were looped together and created a knot. And then another. And another. Until a length of twisted fibres was transformed into a knotted textile.

It's deceptively straightforward that the words 'knitting' and 'knotting' are essentially the same, and appear as *cnyttan* or 'to tie with a knot' in Old English, *knytja* in Old Norse, and as *knütten* in Middle Low German. The reality is, however, that the history of 'knitting' is a little more complex than it first appears.

To unravel the mystery we have to go back to some of the earliest 'knitted' textiles that have been uncovered – the world's oldest socks (see THE HISTORY OF CRAFTED CLOTHING, pages 120–121). Known as Coptic socks, these ancient artefacts date

back to sometime between A.D. 100 and 400 and were discovered, wonderfully preserved, in various Egyptian tombs. They're beautiful things. Like big, gloriously bold bed socks in bright colours, these foot coverings have just two toes (so they could be worn with thonged sandals) and were made from touchably soft, spun wool.

At first, these Coptic socks were thought to be the earliest examples of knitting, but in the painstaking process of trying to recreate the socks, textile historians discovered that they were, in fact, made using a different, much older technique known as NÅLEBINDING.

So what's the difference? To the outsider, the results of nålebinding and knitting look similar and yet they're created in two very different ways. Knitting uses one long, continuous strand of yarn arranged in a series of interlocking loops; each loop not only links to the loops either side of it, but also to the loops in the rows above and below it. In theory, you can pull one end of the yarn and the whole knitted textile will unravel. To knit, you usually need two or more needles.

Nålebinding is a much older technique. As with knitting, you create a textile from interlocking loops of yarn, but to make a loop you 'sew' the yarn through the loops you want to interlock with rather than pull one loop through another. Not only does this mean you need just one small needle, instead of two long ones, but it also means you can get away with using shorter lengths of yarn, as the entire length has to be passed through every stitch.

Interestingly, nålebinding translates literally to 'needle binding' in Danish, and it's in Denmark that many of the oldest examples pop up. Tybrind Vig was a Mesolithic fishing village populated between about 5400 and 4000 B.C. Because of sea level changes over the years, the site was slowly submerged under water and only rediscovered back in the 1970s. Being underwater created challenges when it came to excavating the site, but it preserved lots of artefacts that would otherwise have rotted away over time, including wooden tools, fishing equipment, textiles, food remains and human burials. There, fragments of nålebinding were discovered, created from vegetable fibres, and were probably fishing nets rather than

clothing. In fact, most of the early examples of nålebinding before 3000 B.C. seem to be parts of nets.

Eventually some bright spark had the idea of using nålebound to make clothes. In fact, it seems lots of bright sparks had the same idea independently. From a 3,000-year-old beret found in China to a jaunty poncho from Peru, a woman's shirt from Denmark and a woolly beanie hat in Germany, nålebound clothes start to appear, across the globe, from about 1500 B.C. onwards.

The Vikings were supreme masters of the art. They made hats, socks, gloves and even sieves, using nålebinding. One of the most famous survivors is known as the 'Coppergate Sock', found in York (once the Viking settlement of Yorvik) in the backyard of a 10th-century building. It's the sole example of nålebinding ever to have been found in England. Whether it was made by a Viking who lived in the settlement or came on the foot of a Scandinavian visitor isn't known.

Nålebinding is a technique that doesn't produce results in a hurry. It's interesting that many of the objects that have made their way into museums were made to cover the body's extremities. Gloves, hats, mittens, socks and bags would not only have kept those key body parts warm, but, as smaller items, would have been manageable in terms of time and effort.

It's amazing to know that nålebinding is still popular today, from hats with ear flaps in Peru to Iranian socks, Scandinavian mittens to African bags.

Knitting, in contrast, seems to have been a relatively late developer. Most textile historians think that, at some point, people realised that if you didn't pull the end of the yarn through each loop, you could keep going with one continuous length. As with nålebinding, many of the early knitted pieces are small items, worked 'in the round' to create cylindrical shapes such as socks, hats and stockings. There's a gorgeous fragment – now in the Victoria & Albert Museum in London – that dates back to sometime around the 12th or 13th century A.D. Knitted from blue and cream cotton, it probably started life as a long sock, but it's the pattern that really catches your eye; with its tiny blue diamonds, white stripes and 'Z' motifs, it's spectacularly familiar and wouldn't look out of place hanging from a 21st-century Christmas mantelpiece.

'Back-and-forth knitting' or 'flat knitting' – the type your granny might do with two needles to create a sweater – doesn't seem to emerge until the medieval period. Few examples of knitting survive from the 14th and 15th centuries; we glean our information from contemporary writings and paintings instead. One religious painting from around 1400, the Buxtehude Altar, for example, shows Mary skilfully knocking up a short-sleeved sweater, while knitted vests are mentioned in a list of items in an English Parliamentary Act of 1552. By the 1600s, knitted clothing had woven itself into all sections of society – from extravagant knitted bishops' gloves, designed to be worn during religious ceremonies, to humble, everyday knitted caps used by working-class men and boys.

Until the Industrial Revolution, knitting was a cottage industry. Hand knitting remained a source of income for many poor families, who could work from home, with no set-up costs, and fit knitting in around other manual work, childcare or seasonal labour. It was also something that women, the elderly and infirm and young children could do, providing the wider family with extra revenue.

Its association with low-income families meant knitting was not considered a respectable craft, unlike PAPER QUILLING (pages 34–35) or DÉCOUPAGE (pages 46–47), for well-do-to ladies. That all changed with Queen Victoria, an avid knitter and crocheter, who promoted both crafts as suitable and fashionable hobbies. She famously made, amongst other items, stockings for her children, bed quilts and eight special 'Scarves of Honour' to be presented to British servicemen fighting in South Africa. In fact, the soldiers' scarves were crocheted and Queen Victoria was probably the first famous person to take up what was at the time a new and groundbreaking craft.

KNITTING

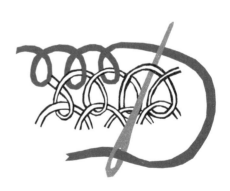

NÅLEBINDING

The origins of crochet are a tangle. As with many textile crafts, there's no definitive starting point. What's interesting is just how late crochet seems to have arrived on European shores, compared to both knitting and nålebinding. We have no solid evidence of the craft being practised in Europe until the 1800s, although many scholars think it may have started life as an EMBROIDERY technique, a bit like chain stitch, called 'tambouring', which used a hooked needle.

A boost to the craft came in the form of a pattern book, published in the 1840s by Eleonore Riego de la Branchardiere, called *Knitting, Crochet and Netting; with twelve illustrations*, which showed thousands of readers how to copy these newfangled crochet techniques. At the same time, over in Ireland, the nation was in the grip of the potato famine. The economy had collapsed, crops failed and the population were starving. In a bid to help, church members and charities offered to teach the new craft of crochet to anyone willing to learn, the idea being that families – especially women and children – could make crocheted items at home to sell and bring in extra income.

Sales were slow at first. Crochet was quick and easy to produce, but seen as a poor relation to LACE MAKING (pages 116–119) and other more expensive textiles. No-one with money, it seemed, wanted to be seen wearing such a 'common' adornment. But then something happened to change all that. Queen Victoria was given a gift of Irish

crochet. She loved it. Not only did she wear it with pride, prompting high society to clamour for this fashionable new product, but Queen Victoria also learned how to crochet for herself and produced hand-made gifts for friends, family and subjects. This act – which removed its stigma as a working-class craft – helped catapult crochet into popular consciousness. Today, knitting and crochet remain two of the most popular and practised of crafts. Both are accessible, requiring little in terms of start-up costs, but perhaps one of their strongest appeals is their sociability. Knitting and crochet are both skills that can be done communally, as part of a group or 'bee', which makes them unique amongst other more solitary crafts. With the modern world often making it difficult either to connect socially or create something tangible, knitting and crochet solve two problems in one. Virtual communities of knitters and crocheters are hugely active – social networks such as Ravelry allow crafters to connect across continents – while exciting offshoots, such as guerrilla knitting groups, have caught the attention of a new generation of crafters interested in combining craft, politics and social change – a phenomenon known as 'craftivism'. The Pussyhat Project, for example, mobilised millions of people to knit and wear bright pink bobble hats as a symbol of solidarity for the inaugural Women's March on Washington in 2017. 'Yarnbombing' comes from a similar motivation – a desire to take something perceived as 'feminine' and turn it on its head – transforming a comfortable craft into politicised, urban graffiti.

CROCHETDERMY

Knitting and crochet have often had a cosy, domestic image, one that some crafters and artists like to subvert to their advantage. UK creative Shauna Richardson uses crochet to form taxidermy-like animal forms and sculptures called 'crochetdermy'. Using a traditional, simple craft, she creates pieces of conceptual art that are both radical and surprising, and yet firmly rooted in an ancient tradition. With just a 3mm crochet hook and mohair yarn, Shauna has crafted a menagerie of creatures, including three 7.6m lions for the London 2012 Olympics, which took the best part of two years to complete and 36 miles of wool.

|||||||||||||||||||||||||||||||||||||||||||||||||||||||||||

DID YOU KNOW?

Crook, hook and crochet all derive from the same origin, the Old Norse *krāka*. This became the Middle English *crok*, meaning 'hook'.

|||||||||||||||||||||||||||||||||||||||||||||||||||||||||||

LACEMAKING

Lace is an example of what is known as an 'openwork' fabric; its structure is essentially like a net, with the spaces making up as much of the design as the threads. While openwork, net-like fabrics have been around for thousands of years, the specific techniques that create lace didn't emerge until the 16th century.

There are two main methods of making lace: one uses a needle and thread (needle lace) to EMBROIDER together hundreds of tiny stitches, the other (bobbin lace) is a technique more akin to plaiting, where lots of threads wound onto bobbins are crossed over each other or twisted to form a pattern. The pattern, which the lacemaker needs to follow, is first drawn onto a piece of PAPER, then pricked with pinholes and laid onto a cushion as a template.

The origins of lacemaking are hotly disputed – both Italy and Flanders lay claim to the prize – but the city of Venice certainly played a pivotal role in its development. In the 16th century, Venice was a thriving trading port and we know it was there that the first bobbin lace pattern book was printed in 1559 – *Le Pompe: Patterns for Venetian Lace*. By 1600, however, exquisite handmade lace was being produced in centres across Europe, including Spain, France and England.

As with many commercially successful crafts, the economic gap between the makers and the purchasers of lace could not have been wider. Lace was painstakingly slow to make and expensive in terms of raw materials – most early lace was made from imported silk, gold, silver and fine linen threads – keeping it well out of the reach of the ordinary man or woman.

‖‖‖

DID YOU KNOW?

In the 1700s, French lace was banned from being imported into England. English high society, desperate to get their hands on contraband goods, took to smuggling lace in increasingly ingenious ways. Records from Customs during this time include lace being smuggled in a pie, under a Turk's turban and, gruesomely, in a coffin; most of the body had been removed, leaving the head, hands and feet behind and the coffin stuffed with hugely valuable Flanders lace.

‖‖‖

Only members of the aristocracy, royalty and the church could readily afford handmade lace. In the mid 1700s, for example, a pair of sleeve ruffles cost over four times the annual salary of a lacemaker. The work was often subject to the whims of political alliances, religious schisms and trade wars; in the 1800s, on the several occasions Britain went to war with France, imports of French lace were interrupted and British lacemakers enjoyed short periods of high demand and inflated wages.

But for most lacemakers throughout history, especially in the 1800s and early 1900s, life was harsh. Lacemaking was often done by impoverished women, who worked in groups not only for companionship but to share the cost of heating and lighting a room by candlelight. During this time, lace schools also emerged. Under the auspices of charity, small schools were established with the express purpose of teaching young children to make bobbin lace to sell, in return for a wage and the opportunity to read. In reality, many of these schools were little more than centres for child labour, exploiting their vulnerable charges by making them work interminably long hours, often under fear of physical punishment, for meagre or no returns.

The Reverend Thomas Mozley, writing in 1857, describes one such lace school in Northamptonshire, England:

On the higher green was the 'lacemaking school,' as it was called. Near thirty children were packed in a small room, and kept at their pillows from six in the morning, all the year round, to six in the evening. They were arranged in groups of four or five, round candles, about which were water-bottles so fixed as to concentrate the light on the work of each child. Girls were sent thither from the age of five, on a small weekly payment... For a year or two the children earned nothing. They could then make a yard of edging in a week, and, deducting expenses, they got twopence for it. By the time they were eleven or twelve they could earn a shilling or eighteenpence a week.

During the early and mid 19th century, the invention of lacemaking machines spelled the end for much of England's handmade lace industry. Manufacturers were keen to find a way to produce lace that was affordable for the mass market, and towns like Nottingham became famous for machine-made lace and exporting lacemaking technology to other countries, such as the United States. The skills of lacemakers haven't been lost, however, thanks largely to groups such as The Lace Guild in the UK, The International Organization of Lace, Inc in America and L'Organisation Internationale de la Dentelle au Fuseau et à l'Aiguille in France, who actively promote the history and techniques of handmade lace, along with the work of skilled amateurs and heritage craft enthusiasts.

THE HISTORY OF CRAFTED CLOTHING

TROUSERS

The world's oldest trousers are also the world's oldest jodhpurs. The 4000-year-old trousers – unearthed at the Yanghai tombs in China's Tarim Basin – are crafted from three sections of cloth, one for each leg and one for a roomy crotch, stitched together using matching thread. The trousers were buried with other horsey accessories – a leather bridle, horse bit and whip – and are thought to have belonged to nomadic, equestrian herders who may have invented modern trousers to cope with long rides. The Yangtai herders were clearly natty dressers – other finds included colourful sheepskin boots, silk scarves, feathered hats, a fringed mini-skirt and a miniature loincloth.

WOOLLY JUMPER

When a Norwegian glacier began to melt, it revealed the oldest KNITTED jumper ever found. The 1700-year-old boatneck sweater – made from soft sheep and lamb's wool – had a diamond twill weave, was light beige and brown, fitted a slim, average height man, and had been lovingly patched on a number of occasions. Radiocarbon dating established that the 'Lendbreen Tunic' had been knitted between 230 and 390 A.D. Interestingly, researchers think the sleeves were added a while after the sweater was first knitted, making this also the world's oldest tank top.

SHOES

The oldest sandals were found in Oregon, USA. The Fort Rock Sandals are about 10,000 years old – made from woven bark – and consist of a flat sole, a toe wrap and ankle twine (a bit like an espadrille). The oldest LEATHER shoe comes from Armenia and is estimated to be around 5,500 years old. Cut from a single piece of tanned leather and shaped to fit the wearer, this rare right shoe would have been stuffed with grass for insulation and the perfect fit for a size 5 foot (US size 7).

SKIRT

Remnants of the oldest surviving skirt were discovered in a south-eastern Armenian cave (along with the world's oldest SHOE – see above). Only scraps remain, but textile historians can piece together that the skirt would have been made from woven reeds and could have belonged to a man or woman.

DRESS

The Tarkhan Dress, a V-neck linen dress or tunic, is the world's oldest complete woven garment. Found in an Egyptian cemetery in 1913, and left unexamined for 60 years, recent radiocarbon tests have dated it somewhere between 3482–3102 B.C. The dress is tailored from three sections of hand-woven striped flax linen, with pleated sleeves and a bodice, and would have probably been worn by a young teenager or a slim woman.

SOCKS

Just before the First World War broke out, English papyrologist John de Monins Johnson began excavating the Egyptian city of Antinooupolis. He was looking for papyrus (see PAPER) but instead found socks. Tossed aside as a 'lesser' find at the time, these two separate socks are now viewed as precious survivors of an ancient civilisation and a comforting reminder that even the Egyptians loved warm cosy toes. Of the two socks found, the oldest dates from around 100-350 A.D. and is thought to have belonged to an adult. The other sock is smaller; a child's left foot, and thought to date to 200-400 A.D. Both socks divide off the big toe, so you can wear them with sandals, and are made from wool, using an ancient technique called NÅLEBINDING (pages 108-113).

UNDERWEAR

When the floorboards of an Austrian castle were lifted during a recent restoration project, you can imagine the archaeologist's surprise at the discovery of a cluster of women's underwear. Among the finds were the earliest bras ever found - four linen bras, dated to around 1400 A.D. Scholars had always wondered what the medieval writers were referring to when they talked about 'breastbags' and now we know. The bras looked exactly like the modern brassiere and were not only functional but prettily decorated with lace and other details.

A pair of string pants also turned up; far from being women's skimpy knickers, however, they are thought to be men's underwear. In fact, from the earliest loincloths to up until the 1800s, it seems that men were the only ones to wear pants. Ötzi's loincloth is one of the oldest ever found (see WEAVING, pages 82-87) but one of the most impressive hauls of men's pants came from the tomb of Tutankhamun, who was entombed with 145 loincloths. It seems you can never have too many spare pants.

JEWELLERY

The oldest piece of bling ever discovered was a 130,000-year-old necklace, found in Croatia. The piece was made from eight eagle talons, polished and notched for stringing together. Scientists discovered that the talons came from three different white-tailed eagles, probably captured alive, which is an astonishing feat in itself. And the most remarkable thing? The necklace was made by a Neanderthal.

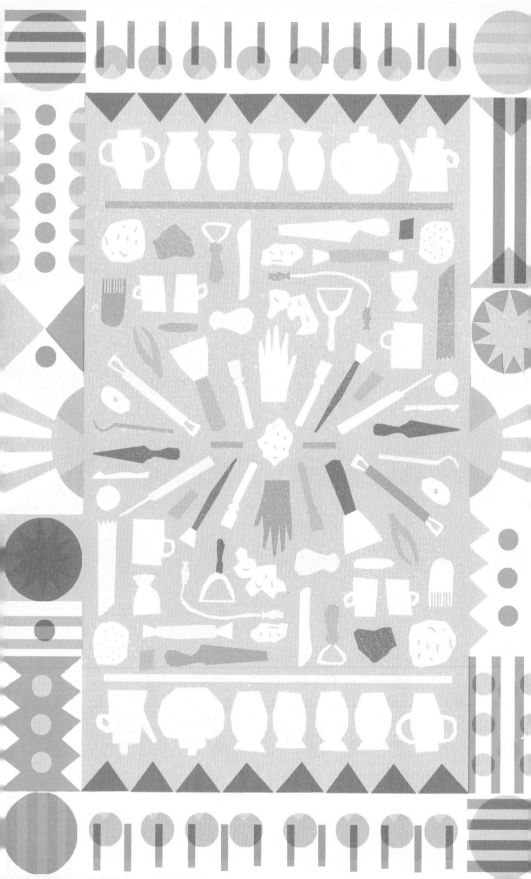

POTTERY,
GLASS
&
STONE

POTTERY

Imagine if the first pottery objects ever made weren't designed to be cooked in or eaten off. Imagine if they were made to be deliberately blown up. That's the theory put forward to try and explain a vast hoard of ancient pottery fragments and figures found at Stone Age sites in the Czech Republic.

The most famous of these sites is Dolni Věstonice, at the foot of the Děvín Mountain. More than 700 figurines were discovered there, including clay models of mammoths, lions and rhinos (all of which would have roamed Ice Age Europe) as well as the Venus of Dolni Věstonice, a sensuous female sculpture dated to 30,000 years ago, making it the oldest fired clay object ever found.

Experimental archaeologists (who test ancient crafts to see how they work) managed to figure out how these clay objects were made – the figures were fired at a relatively low temperature (500–800°C) and made from local clay soil mixed with crushed mammoth bone. What's even more fascinating is that they suspect our Stone Age potters were deliberately making the pottery explode by keeping the clay very wet and placing it in the hottest part of the fire. It seems the process of making and the act of breaking was more important than the finished object itself.

It's impossible to say which members of the group were potting. In the past, the Venus and other prehistoric sculptures of the female form were interpreted as erotic art made by men, for the pleasure of men. More recent interpretations have suggested that women could have been at the centre of the craft process, creating figures for rituals where females formed part of the spiritual elite. Interestingly, a recent re-examination of the Venus of Dolni Věstonice found traces of a small fingerprint. This fingerprint is too petite to have belonged to a man – it's either a woman's or a child's – and forces archaeologists to reconsider our traditional ideas about the roles of women and younger members of the group in the distant past.

For the oldest pots, rather than figurines, known in the world, you have to come forward ten thousand years. Bucketfuls of pottery fragments were found in Xianrendong cave in southeast China, the oldest dating to around 20,000 years ago. This discovery is interesting as it challenges two previously held assumptions on pots; that people only started to make pots with the advent of farming 12,000 years ago (it's assumed that farmers suddenly needed pottery vessels to carry water for their crops and that pots were too cumbersome for hunter-gatherers to take with them) and that those first pots were developed to carry liquids. It's now believed that the first known pots were made for cooking in rather than transporting water or eating from.

The pottery remnants at Xianrendong were probably crude pots and bowls, smoothed on the outside with grass. They also bear evidence of scorch marks and soot, indicating that they were used for cooking food on an open fire. But why start cooking food all of sudden, when humans had been managing perfectly well for thousands of years on a diet of raw food? One suggestion is that 20,000 years ago, Earth was in the grips of the coldest part of the last Ice Age. The prolonged freeze could have caused food shortages among hunter-gatherer groups. Cooked starch, fat and protein yielded more energy than the same raw food and allowed some of the nutrients to be more readily absorbed. In other words, you could eat less food but still extract the same calories.

And what were our early chefs rustling up in their cooking pots? Food analysis there, and at another similar site, revealed traces of wild birds (including cranes, ducks, geese and swans), boar, deer, tortoise, fish, shellfish, small mammals, plums and wild rice.

Another idea is that hunter-gatherer groups were forced into close proximity by the advancing ice sheets and harsh climate. Denser populations might have created the right conditions for new crafts, such as POTTERY and WEAVING (pages 82–87), to emerge and spread. Either way, it doesn't take too long for good ideas to disseminate. So, sometime between 20,000 and 14,000 years ago, the skill of making pots crept across East Asia and into the Middle East. By 14,500 B.C. it appears in Japan, in Persia by 8000 B.C. and on the Indian subcontinent by 5500 B.C. Even further afield, pots pop up in the archaeological record around the same time: in the Americas by 5500 B.C. and in sub-Saharan Africa by 9500 B.C. Whether these pot makers worked out the technique by themselves or were taught the craft by an 'outsider' remains unknown. It's also interesting that, in many instances, the archaeology tells us that the craft of potting would 'arrive', be used for a period and then be lost, only to return hundreds or even thousands of years later.

It's worth mentioning that pottery never really took off in Australia, even though the indigenous tribes in the north would probably have known the craft through contact with Indonesian fisherman. One theory is that the Aboriginals, despite knowing and valuing clay for ceremonial painting, had no real use for clay pots.

They already had everything they needed. Water was transported in wood containers and woven baskets worked perfectly well for storing and carrying food. It's telling that, when Europeans settlers did bring ceramics and glass to Australia, the indigenous people found their own ways to use them, including turning broken shards into spear points and cutting tools.

Early pots were simple but it's important to recognise just how much knowledge prehistoric potters would have needed to make and successfully fire pottery. First, the potter would have needed to find a source of suitable local clay. He or she would have also known that, to stop the pot cracking when it was fired, it was a good idea to add a handful of sand, crushed bone or shell to the mix. The potter would have also been required to build and maintain a bonfire or fire pit hot enough to 'cook' the pot, not just dry it out – clay only starts to change its chemical composition at about 500°C and sudden changes in the bonfire's temperature could cause the pot to crack. Our prehistoric crafters would have also worked out that pottery vessels with rounded, bag-like bottoms were less likely to crack than pots with hard angles, and so took great pains to smooth off or decorate the outside of their work as an extra flourish.

‖‖‖

DID YOU KNOW?

Japan's oldest pottery is around 16,500 years old and called 'Jomon', which means 'rope patterned'; makers would press ROPE (pages 104–105) into the soft clay to make their pots look like WOVEN baskets. Most Jomon vessels were used for boiling and cooking, but recent research has discovered that these early potters also used their pots to store the dead bodies of very young children.

‖‖‖

THROWN POTTERY

One key invention, however, seems to have taken a very long time to arrive: the pottery wheel. It's incredible to think that such a fundamental piece of human technology emerged so much later than other 'inventions', including the NEEDLE (pages 74–75), WEAVING (pages 82–87), boats, farming and even making musical instruments. Yet it's probably thanks to pottery that we have a wheel in the first place.

Early potters' wheels were actually more like 'Lazy Susans' or turntables, which were spun by hand to facilitate the making of a pot. The clay wasn't designed to be worked at speed, like the modern potters' wheel, and the wheel itself would have probably been made from baked clay, stone or wood, pivoting on a peg. Despite the fact that these wheels were probably in common use across broad stretches of the Middle East, Far East and into parts of India from as early as 5000 B.C., the idea of putting a wheel on a wagon or chariot seems to take another 1,500 thousand years (see WHEELWRIGHTING, pages 192–193).

In today's craft world, pottery remains one of the most popular and commercial of all the artisan traditions. For all the reliability and uniformity of factory-made ceramics, few things evoke the human spirit as much as a hand-made pot, with its delicious imperfections and maker's thumbprints. Today, the ceramics community is more vibrant and connected than at any other time, thanks in large part to internet sites such as Etsy and Instagram, which give makers a chance to both connect with, and sell to, a wide customer base, and TV shows such as the BBC's Great Pottery Throw Down. For the proactive consumer, behind-the-scenes footage, virtual studio tours and posts of work-in-progress give an unprecedented glimpse into the personalities and creative processes of the crafter, helping buyer and maker connect. There are also large-scale events for the discerning craft buyer, which allow makers and potential customers to meet in person, chat and browse on an informal, informed

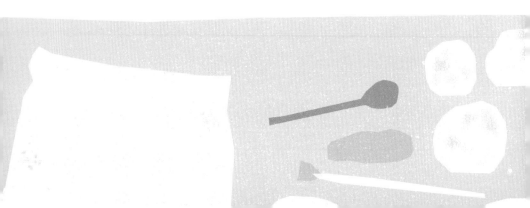

a yearly gathering that brings together over 100 potters from the UK, Europe, Australia and Japan to 'Meet the potters, talk pots, and buy direct from the maker.'

Vogue recently described pottery as the new yoga, claiming it had 'crept out of the knick-knack shop and into the realm of fashion'; the cult status of this ancient and humble craft seems to lie in its messy, unpretentious process – providing the tech-weary with a chance to literally reconnect with the earth. It's also wonderfully unpredictable – a quality that forces the maker to slowly read, react to and understand the material they're working with. Many have compared pottery to meditation – with its need to switch off certain parts of the brain and engage others – while others love the idea of making or owning a one-of-a-kind object that they will use and engage with everyday.

PORCELAIN

Throughout history, most pottery was fired at low temperatures. From early medieval Islamic lustreware to Italian Renaissance Maiolica, potters created a vast array of colourful, beautiful and useful pots relying on kilns that would reach no higher than about 1200°C. That is, apart from the Chinese.

Chinese potters were streets ahead of everyone else; as early as 1600 B.C., improvements in kiln design, fuel mixes and firing techniques allowed pottery to be fired at much higher temperatures – nearer 1400°C. Along with the discovery of large natural deposits of a pure white clay called kaolin, these very high temperatures allowed China, over the next two millennia, to race forward in the production of a new, exciting technology – porcelain. From the moment Marco Polo first brought porcelain back from China in the 14th century, Europe fell instantly, madly in love with this exotic, translucent material. Desperate to copy the Chinese technique, European potters tried and failed to master the secrets of true porcelain making – they simply couldn't figure out the recipe.

The formula was finally cracked at the beginning of the 18th century, thanks in large part to an extravagant and larger-than-life character, King Augustus of Poland. Augustus was a passionate collector of porcelain (amassing over 35,000 pieces in his lifetime) and set out to discover its closely guarded secrets. Europeans had been trying for nearly three centuries to recreate the process but it was only when Augustus imprisoned a young alchemist, Johann Friedrich Böttger, and forced him to uncover the formula, that Europe finally managed to produce its own version of porcelain. The production of porcelain at the Meissen factory, near Dresden, got underway in 1710 and became one of the most famous names in pottery history. It's still going strong today.

GLAZING

The earliest pots were porous. The low firing temperature resulting from an open fire, combined with the lack of any type of glaze or shiny finish, meant that most prehistoric pottery would slowly absorb some of its liquid contents. This has proved useful to archaeologists, who've been able to deduce what kinds of things people ate and drank from their pots, but it would have been pretty frustrating for the pottery owner who could never enjoy the benefits of an entirely waterproof container.

That's where glazes come in. A glaze is a thin layer of glass or lustrous coating that's applied to a clay object before it's fired. It's beneficial for two reasons: first, a glaze can make a porous pot waterproof – perfect if you want to use it for food and drink – and second, depending on what you add to the glaze, it can become a fundamental part of the decoration of a pot.

The first glazes were probably a mistake. Or, perhaps more accurately, a happy accident. Imagine our prehistoric potter firing his or her bowl in a fire pit. The hole had been dug in sandy soil or on a beach and then the fire built and lit. Once the fire had died down, the potter might have noticed something interesting in the ashes at the bottom – that some of the sand, saturated with salt water, had melted and hardened into a glossy substance. At what point potters began deliberately trying to recreate this process, we don't know. Some of the earliest glazed objects date back as far as 5000 B.C. and were made

with something called 'Egyptian paste' or Egyptian faience. When heated, this mixture of silica (sand) and alkaline salts transformed into a gloriously bright glass-like material, which the Ancient Egyptians absolutely loved; they were captivated by its gleaming, turquoise blue hue – a colour closely linked with Egyptian ideas about fertility and rebirth – and transformed it into beads, temple offerings, scarabs, amulets and tiny funerary statues of gods and animals.

Egyptian paste was an unusual material because the glaze was mixed into the fabric of the object. Most glazes are applied to the surface of an already-fired pot and then fired again. The development of glazes goes hand-in-hand with improvements in firing technology and the ability to reach higher temperatures. What's interesting about glazes is just how many variables are at play and, over time, people have realised that tinkering with these variables can produce hugely different results. Potters can experiment with firing temperature, how much oxygen is in the kiln, minerals and inorganic compounds in the glaze and many other factors to produce a vast array of pottery types. Potters found, for example, that adding lead (see POISONOUS CRAFTS, pages 226–227) to a glaze meant it could be fired at a lower temperature or that if they incorporated tin oxide, they could turn a see-through glaze pleasingly opaque.

RAKU POTTERY

Most pots are fired over a long period. The kiln starts off cold with the pots inside, slowly heats up, reaches its desired temperature and then slowly cools down again. Only when the kiln is cold will the finished pots be removed. The whole firing, cooling and unloading cycle can take two to three days.

Raku is an ancient Japanese technique that's short and sweet. Pots are often loaded into a preheated kiln, fired for a brief time (only minutes in some cases) and then removed from the kiln whilst they are still glowing hot. The pot is then placed in a container with combustible materials, such as sawdust or newspaper. The interaction between the glaze and the carbon-rich atmosphere gives rise to a wonderfully unpredictable set of colours, effects and surfaces on the pots – such as crackling, metallic glazes and black unglazed areas.

While the original technique was devised for simple, handmade beakers designed for tea ceremonies, when raku firing came to the West in the 1950s, modern potters adapted the process for decorative pieces and embraced the technique for its random, 'lucky-dip' results and quick firing. The father of Western raku, ceramist Paul Soldner, encouraged fellow potters to look for the creative opportunities in raku's

unpredictability, believing that 'mistake, rather than necessity was the mother of invention.' Raku firing is not, however, entirely unsystematic. Contemporary potters, such as David Roberts, have mastered the technique to such an extent as to turn raku firing into an art form, enjoying the delicate balance between control and uncertainty.

SGRAFFITO

In Italian *sgraffito* means 'to scratch'. This decorative process involves the potter applying layers of colour to the pot and then scratching patterns into these layers, revealing the clay underneath. Its origins are long debated – and may go back as far as the 10th century – but the technique was mastered and perfected by potters in both the Middle East and Italy. In fact, most European countries have a tradition of sgraffito decoration. In England, for example, it was known as 'scratch ware' and North Devon pottery, which was renowned for its bold sgraffito decoration, was traded in vast quantities with America during the 17th century in return for tobacco. In 1935 archaeologists working in Jamestown, Virginia, discovered a huge collection of sgraffito pots dumped in a drainage ditch. Once washed clean and analysed, the pots turned out to have been made around 1670 and sailed all the way from the south coast of England, destined for the colonial market. Interestingly, sgraffito is once again a popular method – partly because it's such a satisfying and forgiving technique as you are working with leather-hard clay, but also because the results are so graphic and pleasingly 'naive'. Modern potters Vicky Lindo Ceramics (a collaboration between Vicky Lindo and Bill Brookes) continue the North Devon tradition, creating their own, hugely inventive version of sgraffito from their Bideford studio.

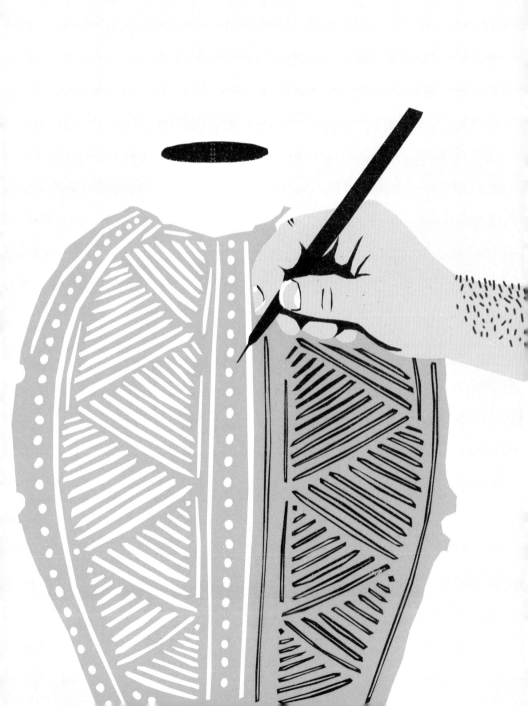

SPONGING

The urge to print, instead of paint, is difficult to resist, especially if you're decorating multiples of things. Sponge printing, where decoration is applied with dabs of a sponge, is nothing new and appears on pottery as early as 2000 B.C., but it was the Victorians – with their love of mass-production – who we most associate with this simple technique. Sponging became popular in the 19th century as a way of getting pattern cheaply onto inexpensive pottery – the bowls, jugs and plates destined for working-class families – and was a cottage industry, often done by children or women working from home.

Ironically, spongeware is now hugely collectible – part in thanks to a revival of the technique by ceramics manufacturers such as the UK's Emma Bridgewater and Nicholas Mosse in Ireland – but also because antique spongeware rarely survived successive decades of robust handling. As a craft, sponging is an easy entry-point into ceramic decoration, a quick way to create a colourful, folk-inspired pot. In recent years, there's been a flurry of decorate-your-own-pot workshops and studios, which encourage people to try techniques such as sponging – often with non-toxic underglazes – for themselves.

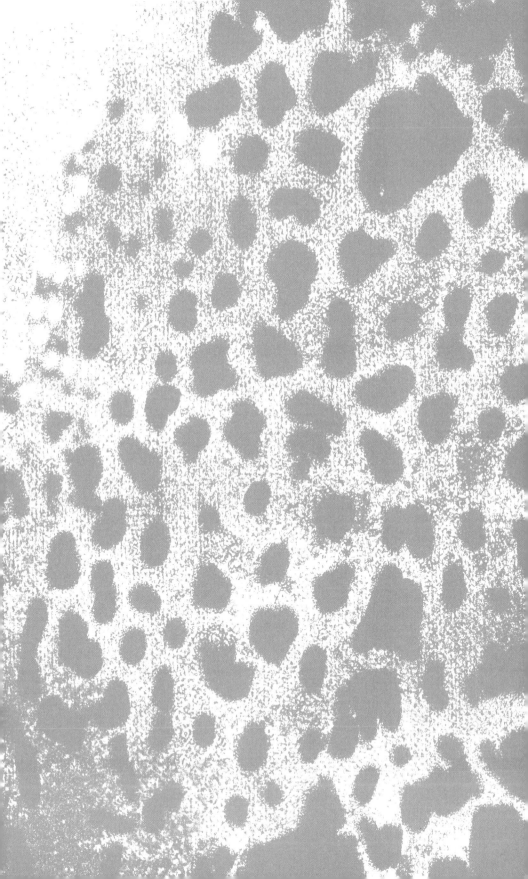

MOSAICS

In 2017, a group of archaeologists and volunteers were just days away from the end of a three-year dig near the village of Boxford, in Berkshire. Funds had all but dried up but then, at the eleventh hour, they struck gold. Or, more specifically, mosaic. They had, in fact, stumbled upon a huge, 1600-year-old Roman mosaic floor, beautifully preserved and lain hidden since the end of the 4th century. It depicts the Greek hero Bellepheron, astride his winged horse Pegasus, Cupid and the Chimera, a fire-breathing beast.

It's an extraordinary find but, to a wealthy Roman householder, this floor decoration would have been par for the course. The floors of many a well-to-do Roman building were richly adorned with mosaics, lavishly illustrating scenes from myth, history and daily life. While some of the more extravagant would have been commissioned from scratch, mosaics in the Roman period were so popular that homeowners could pick a design 'off the shelf' and have it created in situ. That said, when the Romans splashed out on mosaics, they really splashed out. The Alexander Mosaic, uncovered in Pompeii, for example, consists of about 1.5 million individual tiles.

It's difficult to know when the first mosaic was created. Mosaics can be made using any number of small pieced materials:

pebbles, shells, stones, clay, glass and glazed tiles. Shells have long been used for decoration and it's easy to conjure up the image of a prehistoric crafter pushing these or animal teeth and river pebbles into soft clay. Some of the earliest dateable mosaics, however, come from the Eanna Temple in Uruk (now southern Iraq), and cover the 5000-year-old walls with cones of coloured clay and stone pushed into wet plaster.

Modern crafters and artists who use mosaics are drawn to its generous possibilities. Some love the permanence of mosaic's traditional materials – glass or ceramic tiles – and enjoy creating work that has an inherent permanence and longevity. Others like its association with city spaces – especially murals and public art – and the idea that mosaics are robust enough to take the rigours of urban living. And, as with many modern crafts, there have been some new and exciting interpretations of an ancient technique. New York artist Jason Middlebrook describes mosaic as a 'skin for sculpture', creating extraordinary 3D Gaudi-esque pieces, while Chicago's Jim Bachor explores materials beyond the traditional tile and mortar. One of this latest pieces, 'Soup Can', incorporated Campbell's tomato soup into his mortar mix while another work, commissioned by Chivas Regal, used 24 smashed whisky bottles in the design.

GLASSMAKING

People have always treasured glass, but perhaps not for the reason you think. Obsidian is a naturally occurring volcanic glass; when you hit it, it breaks evenly into sharp edges and flakes. More than a million years ago, very early humans knew this and prized obsidian for its ability to cut things. Only recently, archaeologists discovered an 'open-air workshop' on an extinct volcano in Armenia; there, from about 1.4 million years ago, *Homo eretus* and, later, *Homo sapiens* made arrowheads, hand axes, blades and other sharp tools in their hundreds of thousands.

But obsidian had one major disadvantage; it didn't occur everywhere. If you wanted some and didn't have your own volcano to hand, you had to travel to collect it or barter for it with people who did. Scientists believe it may be one of the earliest items ever traded between long distances. Even as far back as 14,000 B.C. we see obsidian travelling between regions as far apart as southeast Turkey and Kurdistan (around 600 miles), a vast distance for people who had yet to invent the wheel or learn to ride horses.

Obsidian wasn't just useful for weapons. The 9000-year-old settlement of Çatalhöyük, in modern-day Turkey, grew rich on its local supply of obsidian; Neolithic crafters carved and polished it into knives, razors, mirrors, jewellery and other beautiful objects both for use at home and to be traded.

When people started experimenting with pottery GLAZES (pages 134–135) or Egyptian paste, it's difficult to understand why they didn't also consider the potential of glass as a material in its own right. Although the earliest glazed objects go back 5000 years, surprisingly, the first solid glass objects don't seem to appear until much later. The date for the first arrival of glassmaking is generally agreed to be about 2500 B.C., in Mesopotamia or Egypt. These early glassmaking pioneers started small, with tiny beads at first, but soon played around with a technique called 'core-forming', where glass is shaped around a removable core. Using this method, glassmakers began to make miniature vases and other small vessels; one of the prettiest and oldest ever found is a tiny blue cosmetic jug, decorated with stylised branches and ancient Egyptian motifs. Sitting in the British Museum, London, this remarkable little make-up container looks as fresh as if it were made yesterday and yet dates to around 1500 B.C. Both men and women wore make-up in ancient Egypt, even after death, and these bottles and their contents would accompany the owner into the afterlife.

For hundreds of years, glass remained a luxury. The glassmaking process was so labour intensive and expensive that only rich customers could afford to buy it. But then a major breakthrough happened. About 50 years before the birth of Christ, glassmakers working in Roman-controlled Syria and Palestine worked out the craft of GLASSBLOWING (pages 146–147). If you took a ball of red hot, molten glass and inflated it like a balloon by blowing down a tube, you could create a whole new range of glass items quicker and more cheaply.

It's no understatement to say that the Romans went on to produce glass on an eye-bogglingly industrial scale. If you could form it from glass, they did. From sculpture to wine storage, mirrors to magnifying glasses, jewellery to bottles, bowls and vases, the Roman world was awash with glass. The quality and colours were breathtaking. Roman glassmakers soon learned how additives, often toxic, could transform a clear material into a dazzling rainbow of hues (see POISONOUS CRAFTS, pages 226–227). They even mastered making window glass, a luxury that, once lost after the fall of the Roman Empire, didn't return to domestic houses in Europe until the 1600s.

GLASSBLOWING

Lots of crafts have an element of showmanship about them, but perhaps none more so than glassblowing. Watching an artisan take a molten ball of glass, puff down a blowpipe and skillfully coax it into a beautiful shape is a spectacle not to be missed; nothing beats that magic combination of peril and deft handiwork.

Glassblowing has been around since the 1st century B.C. and remained the predominant way of forming glass until the late 1800s. It's a brilliantly simple idea – inflating glass to form shapes – and yet hugely skilled. Glass is a flexible but unforgiving medium – one mistake and it's ruined – but perhaps that's where the pleasure and prestige of glassblowing reside. Few things must be as satisfying as transforming an angry mass of hot glass into an object of breathtaking clarity and delicacy.

Its usefulness aside, blown glass has enormous potential for decoration and, apart from niche industries such as handmade window glass, most modern glass blowers explore it for its artistic potential. Bermuda-born Laura Smith, for example, creates high-end glass lighting and interior accessories by layering blown glass with precious metals, while French-

Lebanese artist Flavie Audi turns glass and silver into gem-like, shimmering sculptures and dazzling geological forms.

The equipment needed for glassblowing is often prohibitively expensive for individual crafters; one of the most attractive elements of the glassblowing world are the collective spaces and shared studios which are often open to the public. Places such as Berlin's Glas e.V., London's Glassblowing and VETRO in Texas are not only hives of craft practice but also places where people can watch glassblowers at work, take classes and buy from makers directly (see MAKERS SPACES, pages 17–20).

NEON BENDING

Glass is so versatile – it can be blown, powdered, cut, cast, painted, kiln formed, worked with a flame and sculpted. It can also be filled with neon gas to create glowing, glorious lettering and images.

Neon signs have been around since the early 1900s; the technology, which involves carefully bending thin, hollow glass tubes, lends itself to text and outlines, and proved the perfect medium for signage and advertising. With its showy, look-at-me aesthetic and association with seedy nightlife, neon didn't make the crossover into the domestic arena until the 1980s when urban living, industrial interiors and commercial salvage were welcomed into the mainstream, and neon lights established themselves as the edgy, slightly kitsch accessory to own.

It's been a rocky road for neon recently. For a while it looked like cheap LED lights and plastic signs would finish off signmakers for good; neon was even branded a 'dying art'. And yet, like a luminous pink phoenix rising from the ashes, neon is once again cool. There's an interesting blend of factors at play: retro Americana – with its heady mix of hope and nostalgia – is hitting a nerve for many people at the moment, especially Stateside; neon has also found itself welcomed as a legitimate material and vehicle for expression, with artists such as Dan Flavin and Iván Navarro taking the art world by storm. People, especially the younger market, are rediscovering the handmade appeal of neon – every bend is meticulously crafted – but there's an alluring whiff of danger too; the proximity of the maker's hands to the cripplingly hot flames, as he or she bends and coaxes the glass tubes into shape, provides plenty of drama for the online viewer or workshop visitor.

The aesthetics also couldn't be more current – neon is so very urban, iconic and wonderfully irreverent. Makers and workshops such as Gods Own Junkyard and Lite Brite Neon are busier than ever. It seems neon has captured the perfect combination of eye-catching craftsmanship and fizzing optimism.

STAINED GLASS

While most homeowners had to put up with draughty glassless windows until the 17th century (windows comes from 'wind holes'), one institution was wealthy enough to indulge their taste for glass – the Church.

Some of the oldest known pieces of stained glass can be found at St. Paul's Church, in Jarrow, a building that dates back to A.D. 681. What's interesting is that, unusually for such an old building, we have a written account of the window being commissioned, thanks to the scribblings of the monk, Bede, who lived at Jarrow during the 700s. In 675, Abbot Biscop – unable to find any English stained glass makers – apparently travelled to Normandy in France to find specialist glaziers who would relocate and work on his new church.

Often thought of as a Christian craft, stained glass was also produced in the Middle East as early as the 8th century; Jābir ibn Hayyān, known as the father of modern chemistry, wrote a book called *Kitab al-Durra al-Maknuna* (*The Hidden Pearl*) in which he describes nearly 50 techniques for making and cutting coloured glass.

Back in the West, in about A.D. 1100, the first DIY craft guide to stained glass was written by a monk, Theophilus, in his book *On Diverse Arts*. Both an artist and a metalworker himself, the techniques he describes would be reassuringly familiar to stained glass makers today:

If you want to assemble simple windows, first mark out the dimensions of their length and breadth on a wooden board, then draw scroll work or anything else that pleases you, and select colours that are to be inserted. Cut the glass and fit the pieces together with the grozing iron. Enclose them with lead and solder on both sides. Surround it with a wooden frame strengthened with nails and set it up in the place where you wish.

Over the next 300 years, stained glass enjoyed a period of spectacular popularity and technical advancement. Huge Gothic cathedrals, with their vast window openings, were the perfect vehicle for stained glass, not only as a means of letting in light but also, more importantly, as a way of teaching Bible stories to a largely illiterate congregation; stained glass windows could reveal the Bible, depicting breathtaking, ethereal images of the saints, characters and lessons of the Christian story.

As a modern craft, stained glass hasn't enjoyed the mass appeal it once had, perhaps falling foul of today's love of fuss-free, plain interiors. Many crafters who work with stained glass spend a good deal of their time repairing and restoring historic windows. The 20th century hasn't been kind to church glass, either through inappropriate or careless renovation work, neglect or successive bombings during the Second World War. Even as recently as 2013, for example, Westminster Abbey replaced a set of windows that had been destroyed in the 1940s with stained glass by artist Hughie O'Donoghue.

Modern stained glass, however, can be as attention-grabbing and life enhancing as any cathedral glazing – a handful of artists and crafters are reinterpreting stained glass for a contemporary audience, using abstract ideas and new techniques with dazzling results. New Yorker Tom Fruin, for example, has steered attention away from religious buildings, focusing on structures altogether more everyday and prosaic,

such as his cabin-like Kolonihavehus, made from brightly coloured plexiglass. Another extraordinary talent, Kehinde Wiley, takes traditional church imagery and reinterprets it to feature contemporary subjects. His spectacular windows, which are made in the Czech Republic and draw on influences from French neo-classical stained glass design, celebrate and challenge ideas about race, gender and identity.

STONE SCUPLTING

Humans like to leave their mark. Creating something permanent isn't just an expression of creativity, it's also one of the ways we can combat our own feelings of mortality. Stone is one of the most enduring materials we have at our disposal and our urge to mark or carve it seems to be a very old one indeed. The earliest examples we have of stone carving are staggeringly ancient, but their purpose is a bit of a mystery. The oldest are 'cupules' or cup stones, little depressions painstakingly chipped out of the surface of a rock face.

They turn up on every continent (apart from Antarctica), but no-one's really come up with a satisfying explanation of what they are. We're also unsure who made them in many instances; dating is tricky but some of the oldest, from two cave sites in central India, may be as old as 500,000 years.

The earliest example we have of a carved stone figure is also extraordinarily old. The tiny statuette of the Venus of Berekhat Ram was found in Israel and, at first glance, looks like a small, lumpy pebble. Archaeologists bickered about whether this was a stone that just so happened to 'look a bit like a woman' or whether someone had deliberately carved grooves in the stone to make it resemble the female form. Later analysis showed it was indeed carved, but the most astonishing revelation was its age – somewhere between 230,000 and 700,000 years old.

Both the cup stones in India and the Venus of Berekhat Ram are simple carvings but we mustn't forget one extraordinary detail; anything that old can't have been made by a modern human. In fact, anything older than 250,000 years old can't even be attributed to Neanderthals. Whoever was carving these early pieces must have been one of our archaic human ancestors, *Homo erectus*. How wrong we were to presume that *Homo sapiens* were the world's only crafters.

But what leaps we have made since those early carvings. The history of art is dominated by classical Greek and Roman statuary, meticulously carved and often remarkably lifelike, while the cathedral masons of the Middle Ages excelled themselves building some of the most complex and awe-inspiring structures ever constructed, combining skills as diverse as craftsman and architect, builder and engineer. What's really impressive, however, are those small-scale societies who built and carved vast stone structures with little more than bare hands and sheer grit. The famous Easter Island heads, for example, in the Pacific Ocean, were crafted between

1000 and 500 years ago using nothing more than stone hand tools and persistence. Nearly 900 statues still exist, some almost 10 metres tall. Experimental archaeologists have spent years trying to fathom how a culture which had no metal chisels, wheels or large animals could carve and manoeuvre such monolithic works.

IIIIIIIIIIIIIIIIIIIIIIIIIIIIIIIIIIIIIIIIIIIIIIIIIIIIIIIIIIIIIIIIIIIII

DID YOU KNOW?

Ancient Egypt was a busy place for stone carvers and one of their most important tasks was to make *shabtis*, tiny funeral dolls that would 'help out' the dead in the afterlife. Each shabti was inscribed with a spell, which the Egyptians believed would bring the doll to life so it could get on with useful chores or provide guidance.

IIIIIIIIIIIIIIIIIIIIIIIIIIIIIIIIIIIIIIIIIIIIIIIIIIIIIIIIIIIIIIIIIIIII

STONEMASONRY

Of all the crafts, stonemasonry is perhaps one of the most physically demanding. While recent advances in technology – such as electric cutting tools and forklifts – have taken some of the grind out of a stonemason's day, the core craft skills have changed little over thousands of years.

There are many different, nuanced divisions within the stonemason's world but the work primarily divides into four groups: one is the fixer, the on-site mason whose job it is to place and fix stone accurately onto a building. Fixer masons travel to jobs to install stone that has been pre-prepared by a banker, the workshop-based mason. He or she specialises in following templates and drawings to shape and dress (finishing) different building components, whether it's a statue plinth or a stone lintel. While some of the banker's work can involve creating details and mouldings, when it comes to intricate figures, foliage and abstract forms, a stone carver is often called in. The US Stone Carvers Guild makes an interesting distinction between the craft of the carver and the artistic sentiments of a sculptor: 'a sculptor assigns shape to an idea. A carver imposes a shape on stone, and must be able to do so reliably and in a manner that can be duplicated.'

The work of the different branches of stonemasonry aren't always mutually exclusive, however. Seasoned stonemasons will often have worked as fixers and bankers over their career, or small firms often have bankers who also can carve. Some practitioners prefer to specialise, such as letter carvers, who focus solely on crafting memorials, commemorative plaques and stone signs by hand.

While stonemasonry may be an ancient craft, it's one that's still fiercely in demand. Whether it's the exquisite letter carving of Britain's Jo Sweeting or the fine figures of stone carver Martin Coward, the drive to preserve ancient buildings and the popularity of stone as a decorative material means that stonemasonry is a craft in robust health. It's also a craft that takes its training seriously. From in-house apprenticeships at cathedrals to college courses, industry training to weekend workshops, it seems there's plenty of good-quality stonemasonry and conservation teaching up for grabs.

WOOD,
WILLOW
&
NATURE

BASKET WEAVING

Few crafts develop in total isolation. Techniques that suit one craft might also prove useful to another, or two crafts may develop together, hand in hand, because they share common methods and materials. In no instance is this truer than weaving. The techniques for weaving fabric are no different from weaving other plant materials – thin strips of bark or grasses, for instance – so when we look for the origins of other crafts, such as willow weaving or basket making, we can look in the same places as textiles.

Remember the clay fragments from the Czech Republic that give us the earliest clues about the origins of fabric WEAVING (pages 82–87)? The same 27,000-year-old bits of pottery also inform us about the origins of basket making. The impressions pressed into the clay fragments show archaeologists that whoever made them had a good grasp of at least two basket weaving techniques: one is open twining, which creates baskets or nets with large spaces between the threads (perfect for sieving things, for example, or catching fish) and closed twining, which creates tightly woven baskets for carrying grain or liquids.

The oldest baskets to have survived the ravages of time come, unsurprisingly, from the arid conditions of Ancient Egyptian tombs. What's clear is just how important baskets were for everyday Egyptian life. With plenty of reed beds and papyrus marshes to exploit, the Egyptians made baskets for all kinds of tasks, from carrying excavated earth to measuring grain. Baskets were the Ancient Egyptian Tupperware, storing everything from food to linen, trinkets to cosmetics. When archaeologists uncovered a 14th century B.C. tomb belonging to a well-to-do couple, Kha and Meryt, they discovered a huge inventory of domestic objects that the happy pair would have used in daily life, including Meryt's hairdressing baskets (which still had hairpins and wooden combs inside), food baskets, and a sturdy basket for keeping architect Kha's tools, including a cubit (see CRAFT INVENTIONS, pages 74–75).

The methods for making these baskets has changed little in the intervening 3000 years; one technique creates a structure by weaving reeds or willow in and out of 'ribs' that form the shape of the basket; the other uses coils of rushes or grasses that are then stitched together. Anyone with a set of retro circular woven placemats or a jute rug will know this technique well.

Many of the traditional rural crafts (see ENDANGERED CRAFTS, pages 22–25) centre around some form of basket

weaving. From the ancient craft of bee-skep (hive) making to lobster pots, swill baskets and winnowing baskets, much of agrarian life was served by the humble basket. Until the last century, the fishing industry alone relied on a rich variety of baskets, each with its own particular weave and design. The names are a delight on the tongue: cockle pads, landing baskets, herring swills, prawn pots, creels, wash maunds, cobbing baskets and kipper drips to name but a few.

Today, many forms of basket weaving are highlighted as 'critically endangered' or 'at risk' by heritage craft organisations (see ENDANGERED CRAFTS, pages 22–25). This may be because there are few people left practising the crafts – they're simply not financially viable – and there are limited training opportunities to pass on skills. Included in this list are swill baskets (baskets made from thin woven strips of oak), Devon maunds (baskets made from wooden splints fixed to a wooden base) and SUSSEX TRUGS (gardening baskets, pages 166–167), and yet, ironically, the craft of basket making as a hobby is thriving. It may not have the cachet of crochet or the multitude of followers that knitting does, but thanks to the work of contemporary

crafters such as Mary Butcher – who explores the creative possibilities of basket weaving – new ways of making are evolving, along with a greater range of materials, including natural sources such as leaves, bark and stems, but also man-made materials like wire, plastic and PAPER.

CORACLE MAKING

When you think of baskets you don't automatically think of sailing, and yet one of the earliest forms of woven object is the coracle, a small one-person, keel-less boat that has been in use since at least the Bronze Age and perhaps even earlier. The coracle is essentially a huge basket covered in waterproof material. It's an ingenious idea, to have something that's buoyant enough to float in just a few inches of water but light enough to carry. The coracle has allowed people the freedom to cross rivers, fish and carry loads over water without the need for any large sailing vessel or access to expensive boat-building materials.

The frame of a coracle was usually made from woven branches, thin laths, or flexible sticks tied together. The earliest coracles were covered with a large hide, then waterproofed with animal fat. By the 17th century, people began experimenting with other coverings, including canvas painted with pitch or wood tar, whereas Asian coracles were made from woven bamboo, often kept watertight with resin or coconut oil, a technique that's still in use today.

Some of the earliest references to coracles and coracle-making go back thousands of years. Stone relief carvings from the 9th century B.C. show Assyrian versions of coracles, called *quffa*, while Herodotus, the Greek historian (circa 450 B.C.), describes shield-like coracles floating down the Euphrates. During his invasion of Britain, Julius Caesar spotted the Celts using seafaring coracles, while an intrepid Irish monk, St. Brendan, may have even sailed to America in a coracle in the 6th century A.D., 500 years before the Vikings were supposed to have landed there and nearly a thousand years before Christopher Columbus. In 1976, adventurer and historian Tim Severin decided to follow St. Brendan's footsteps and prove that it was possible to sail from Ireland to America in a coracle. Using traditional design and building techniques he built the vessel, christened it 'Brendan' and set sail. One year and 4500 miles later Severin, to everyone's amazement, reached the shores of Newfoundland.

Archaeology has pushed the date for coracles even further back in time. A chance discovery at a farm in Fife, Scotland, revealed the cemetery of an early Bronze Age tribe. Further examination revealed that in three of the burials, the coffins were actually made from coracles. Animal skins covered the coracles, traces of fish were present and remnants of a paddle were found. What's amazing is that the shape and dimensions of the coracles were almost identical to those still used in Wales today. And the date of these ancient coracles? 4000 years old.

There seems to be something about these little, gracefully simple sailing vessels that has captured the imagination. Coracle-making workshops in the UK, such as those offered by the Weald and Downland Living Museum or Small Woods, are quickly filled and offer the would-be crafter a chance to not only make a coracle but also take it for a spin. A coracle can be built over two days – the perfect timespan for a weekend course – and many also give the nervous first-timer boater a chance to learn how to row using one oar.

TRUGMAKING

Perhaps one of the most iconic baskets is the trug. It's an enduring symbol of English bucolic life – genteel vegetable gardening and cut flowers – but its origins are very much as a working man's basket. The trug's sturdy but lightweight, rectangular design made it ideal for lots of different agricultural and domestic tasks – sowing grains, feeding livestock, harvesting fruit and vegetables – and came in a nine sizes. The smallest size, No. 1, was a tiny one-pint basket for nuts, berries and eggs, while the vast No. 9 bushel trug could hold the equivalent of eight gallons.

DID YOU KNOW?

Trugs became a must-have garden accessory thanks to Queen Victoria. She had been so impressed by the examples she saw on display at the 1851 Great Exhibition that she placed a large order of trugs as gifts to family members.

Today, you can buy rough imitations of the trug, cheaply put together in China, but the genuine article still comes from Sussex, a county rich in native sweet chestnut and cricket bat willow (*Salix alba* 'Caerulea'), both essential trug components. Sweet chestnut, split into strips, makes up the handle and rim of the trug, a skilled process that involves cleaving the wood and then steaming it into shape. The body of the trug is made from more strips of wood – willow this time – which are soaked or steamed to make them supple and then bent and pinned with copper tacks. Each stage takes time and a careful hand. It can take months to grasp the various techniques, and years to perfect them; both sweet chestnut and willow are also notoriously tricky to work with. It's perhaps not surprising, therefore, that there are only a handful of workshops – such as the Cuckmere Trug Company and Thomas Smith – still making true Sussex trugs in the traditional way.

The earliest reference to trug-making can be found in court documents dating back to 1485, where a Richard Acres describes himself as a 'trug maker'. But the origins of the word suggest an earlier life; 'trug' comes from the Anglo Saxon *trog*, meaning hollow vessel, trough, small boat or basin. It's a word that pops up all over the historical record – as *tråg* in Swedish, *trog* in Icelandic and even *trogolo* in Italian. (Rather wonderfully the 8th-century word for a cot or cradle was *cild-trog* or 'child trough').

From its earliest incarnations to relatively recently, trugs have remained an essential part of rural working life. During both the First and Second World Wars, for example, trugs were so vital to the agricultural economy that trug makers were designated a reserved occupation, making them exempt from military service.

WILLOW WEAVING

In a waterlogged pit on a Roman site just outside Oxford, archaeologists found an interesting selection of ancient artefacts. Among those objects was a leather shoe, a cow skull, a wooden writing tablet and an almost complete drum-shaped wicker basket. Nothing terribly exciting you might say. Yet two things caught the attention of the archaeologists. Firstly, the basket had been deliberately damaged before it had been buried. Second, the willow used to weave the basket was much narrower and finer than any willow available today.

Those two clues have opened up interesting avenues of discussion for craft historians. Our little willow basket was probably used as part of a sacred ceremony; ancient scholars often refer to basket-carrying maidens and religious rites, and deliberately stabbed or burned baskets have turned up at other temple excavations. What's more, the standards of Roman, Greek and Etruscan willow weaving were astonishingly high.

It wasn't just the 'classical' cultures who mastered willow weaving; the oldest example of willow weaving ever found was a fishing net discovered in Finland. The net and other fishing tackle had sunk to the bottom of a lake, most likely the result of a boat capsizing sometime in the distant past. The remarkable fact was its antiquity; this unassuming fisherman's net was about 10,500 years old.

Willow only grows in the cooler regions of the northern hemisphere. Until the middle of the last century, countries who could cultivate willow relied on it heavily for almost every aspect of daily life. From food baskets to coal storage, cradles to fishing pots, willow baskets were everywhere. Willow hurdles, wattle and daub walls, chair seats, fences and fish traps demonstrate how whole communities and areas thrived on the cultivation and manipulation of willow.

Take Vallabrègues, in southern France; only a small village but a huge producer of woven willow since 1247. Between November and May, half the village (men, women and children) would live among the willow beds in rudimentary shelters, where they would harvest and strip the willow. Come the summer, the workers would return to the village and start making baskets. Almost every industry needed their willow products: bakers, butchers, wine growers, florists, shipping, fishermen, olive farmers and many other trades. The last willow weaver ceased working in Vallabrègues in 1980, but the village still holds an annual festival to re-enact the return of the workers from the reed beds.

Today, the ubiquity and cheapness of plastic has taken a scythe to the craft of willow weaving, especially basket making, but a few proponents of the trade are still fighting their corner. Thanks to a renewed interest in a more natural, rustic approach to gardening and the more aesthetically minded grow-your-own movement, willow hurdles, obelisks and other garden structures are enjoying a resurgence. Courses in willow crafts – especially willow sculpture, basket making, living fences and willow archways – are also popular, not only with budding gardeners but also people interested in heritage crafts and traditional rural industries.

THATCHING

Just after the end of the Second World War, in North Yorkshire, a local man came across a flint blade in a field and started digging. Over the following years, find after find emerged from the site now known as Star Carr, including elaborate head-dresses made from deer skulls and antlers, and beautiful beads, but the most exciting discovery was the remnants of the oldest house in Britain.

This 11,000-year-old home would have belonged to the first group of settlers to return to Britain after the end of the last Ice Age, at a time when the country was still joined to continental Europe. The circular timber structure, 3.5 metres in diameter, was probably covered in thatched reeds, a technique that has remained unchanged since. Throughout the Iron Age, Roman occupation, medieval times and even the Industrial Revolution, thatching has remained, to a greater or lesser extent, the quintessentially British house-building craft. For centuries, most cottages and farm buildings in Britain were thatched. Until the Middle Ages, even churches and large houses used thatch. In 1300, for example, records show that six acres of rush were used to roof the hall and chambers at Pevensey Castle, Sussex.

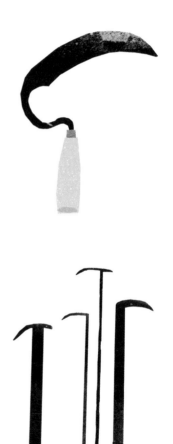

As a building material, thatch made perfect sense. Lightweight and inexpensive, thatching used whatever materials grew locally. In the UK, heather was the material of choice for Scotland and moorland England, water reed throughout Norfolk, combed wheat reed in the West Country and wheat straw in southern England. Each type of thatch produced different architectural results; water reed created angular lines and straight edges, while combed wheat reed lent itself to rounded hips and curved eaves. Heather was used on low, arched roofs and held in place with ropes; wheat straw was 'shaggier' and often needed netting to prevent damage by birds.

Thatching, however, had two main issues to contend with. The first was flammability, especially in crowded towns and cities. In 1173, William Fitzstephen wrote a gushing account of London life, citing only two main faults, 'the immoderate drinking of foolish sorts and the frequency of fires'. Over time, London experienced a number of serious fires - from Boudicca's revolt in A.D. 60 (see TIMBER FRAMING, pages 196–199) to the Great Fire of 1135 – so it came as little surprise when, in 1212, a total ban on new thatched buildings came into force. Any existing thatched houses had little more than a week to plaster over their roofs or face demolition. Other towns and cities soon followed suit.

The second threat to thatching came later, in the form of the Industrial Revolution. The introduction of canals and then railways, which both criss-crossed the UK, allowed mass-produced roof tiles and slates to be easily and economically transported. Thatch was also predominately a rural material, used in the countryside because it was cheap and freely available. Thanks to an agricultural recession at the end of the 1800s and rural populations moving to cities for work, the number of thatched properties gradually declined, as did the number of professional thatchers.

Today, the craft is at an interesting junction. There are still at least 60,000 thatched buildings that need maintaining in Britain alone, about 75 per cent of those are listed. (In the UK, a building is 'listed' when it's of special historic or architectural interest and considered worth protecting.) Enlightened developers are also using thatch on new builds and eco-houses, especially in regions where there is already a strong vernacular tradition. In the 1950s, thatching was an ENDANGERED CRAFT (pages 22–25), there were only around 300 thatchers left in the UK, many nearing retirement age. Thanks to a supply of work from private homeowners, builders and heritage bodies, however, thatching is back in business, with around 1,000 people working in the craft and dozens joining the profession each year.

WOODWORKING

As well as the oldest house in Britain (see THATCHING, pages 170–173), ongoing excavations at Star Carr, the Stone Age settlement, also revealed the earliest evidence of carpentry that we have in Europe. When the site was occupied by families – 11,000 years ago – it would have been at the edge of a huge lake, long since vanished. The residents had decided to build a raised platform or walkway, 30 metres along the shoreline, made from planks split from a much larger section of tree. To do this, they would have had to hammer wedges into the tree trunk, splitting the wood along the grain. The planks would then have been carefully smoothed and shaped using an adze, a tool similar to an axe, with a blade (in their case, a flint blade) at right angles to the handle. The technology sounds crude by modern standards, but these carefully prepared planks represent a huge investment of time and effort by whoever made them, and challenges the idea that it was only thousands of years later, when farming began, that people bothered to create permanent structures and settlements.

But the Star Carr site pales into comparison when we look for the oldest evidence of woodworking in the world. For that, we have to travel back much, much further in time. One and a half million years, give or take. The location is Tanzania, east Africa, where archaeologists managed to unearth ancient stone hand axes belonging to early humans, *Homo erectus*. Under the microscope scientists could see the tiny residues of hardwood on the edges of the stone tools, probably from acacia trees, and the unmistakable wear patterns of heavy-duty woodworking. And what were these early carpenters making? Spears.

From these humble beginnings, humans mastered the craft of woodworking

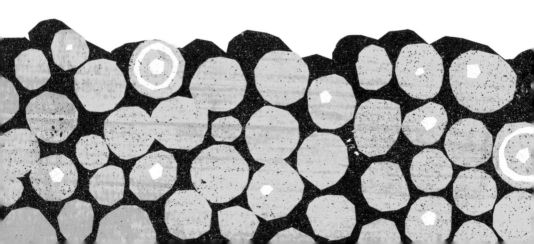

and turned it, in many cases, into an art form. Perhaps few cultures showed such technical prowess in woodworking as the Ancient Egyptians. Much has been made of the lavish, elaborate finds from this era – the gold, the jewellery, the exquisite statues – and yet, if you're passionate about craft, the story of Egyptian woodworking is just as rich. One of the most interesting finds to come from this period is perhaps, at first glance, a bit ordinary; a plywood coffin dating from 3000 B.C. For anyone familiar with woodwork and its techniques, however, this ancient box is a masterclass in sophisticated carpentry.

Writing in 1934 in excitable detail, one observer described the scene:

[The coffin] was discovered last winter in an alabaster sarcophagus in the step pyramid at Saqqara. The burial had been pillaged anciently and the robbers had left the sarcophagus, and probably also the coffin, uncovered.

Both the sides and bottom of the coffin consisted of six-ply wood, each layer being about four millimetres thick and from four to thirty centimetres wide. The layers of wood were arranged alternately in different directions... At the lower corners...each layer of wood...was bevelled at the join, and the inside of each of the four corners was strengthened with wooden bars. The different pieces of wood forming the same layer were fastened together by means of mortise and tenon joints, the tenons...being held in position with wooden pegs. The different layers of wood were also pegged together. The outside of the outermost layer of wood bore a ribbed pattern and had originally been covered with sheet gold fastened in place with gold rivets. The gold, however, had been ripped off by the robbers, and only a few fragments and a few rivets were left.

This one, unique find demonstrates just how skilled the carpenters of Ancient Egypt were. How did they create such thin sheets of different timbers, only millimetres thick,

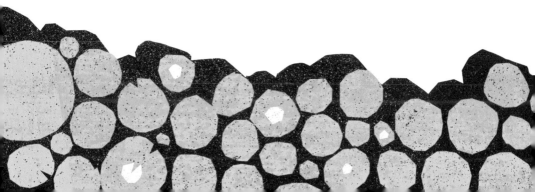

without machinery? How did they know that layering timber at different angles makes it incredibly strong and resistant to movement? How did they know how to create bevels, mortice-and-tenon joints, and wooden pegs? Again, all skills of a sophisticated woodworker.

Perhaps of all the crafts, woodworking has played a fundamental role in the daily life and development of entire civilisations. Timber is useful to so many different groups – from hunter-gatherer societies to complex urban settlements – and can be crafted into an almost infinite number of useful and decorative objects. From the life-sustaining basics such as spears, digging sticks, paddles, spoons, boats, shelter and so on, to the elaborate extravagance of temples, statues and ritual objects, timber can be carved, sliced, bent, steamed and shaped at the carpenter's will, and yet retains the strength and longevity needed for vast structures and load-bearing transport.

Wood is the ultimate raw material. It's structurally very strong, naturally insulating, easy to work, sustainable, simple to procure, fast to build with, and, in many cases, remarkably long lasting. It also happens to be an easy-to-carve,

biddable material, capable of being crafted with breathtaking intricacy and detail. It's perhaps not surprising that in many cultures, historically, carpenters and carvers were often revered crafters, surrounded by myth and religion. From Jesus and Joseph in the Bible to Lu Ban, Chinese patron saint of carpentry, Greek hero Epeius and his Trojan horse, to the Finnish legend Väinämöinen and his boat, great feats of woodworking lay at the heart of many cultures' ideas about themselves. In fact, a motif that pops up time and time again is the idea of 'god as craftsman' (*deus faber*), often a carpenter. In China, for example, the first being, Pangu, is often depicted as a carpenter, carving out the world with his chisel and hammer. Similarly, in Australian aboriginal mythology, Mangar-kunjer-kunja is a lizard god who carved out humans from a wooden lump and then whittled their ears, mouths and noses with his knife.

Today, carpentry and the skill of the woodworker still capture the imagination. Thanks to a handful of excellent books which explore ideas about craftsmanship and the philosophy of making, a new generation has become interested in

woodwork. Modern classics, such
as Richard Sennett's *The Craftsman*,
Ole Thorstensen's *Making Things Right*
and Peter Korn's *Why We Make Things
and Why It Matters*, reveal just how
enriching and important carpentry is.
There's no longer the belief that working
with your hands is the antithesis of intellect;
people who work with wood, and any other
craft medium, know that using your hands
not only gives you space and time to
think, but also that the careful handling
of materials involves every part of your
brain. Each crafted object is a thought
made into substance.

Woodworking is also no longer solely a
man's game. Thanks to trailblazers such
as Amy Umbel and Ariele Alasko in the
US, Anja Sundberg in Sweden, and JoJo
Wood in the UK, female woodworkers
have become an integral part of the
craft community.

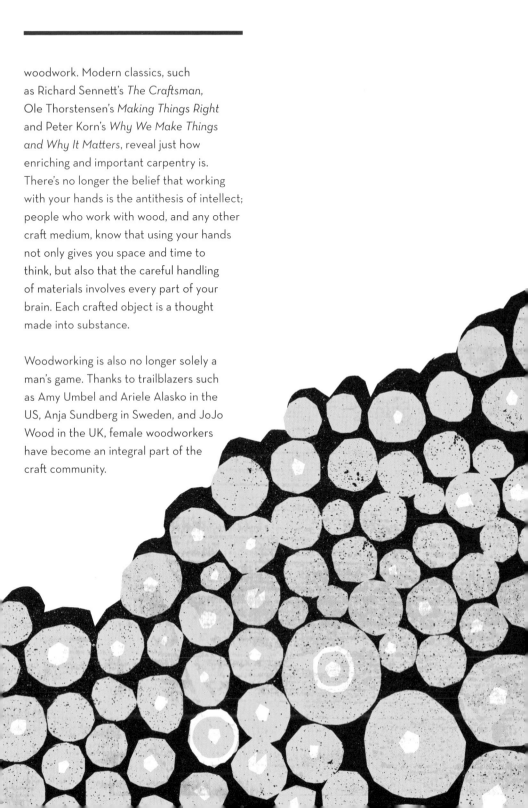

WOODCARVING

One area of woodworking that has really caught the imagination in the past few years is woodcarving. Unlike many of the more involved, apprenticeship-based wood crafts, such as furniture making, there's an ease of access to woodcarving that has encouraged many people who otherwise might have not felt able to have a go. The qualifications are simple; anyone who can safely use a sharp knife can attempt the basics of carving. That's not to say that woodcarving isn't skilled. Anyone who knows timber will recognise the constant challenges of working with a living material. Not only does timber have a tendency to crack, but it also moves, swells and shrinks depending on humidity and temperature.

Some of the oldest 'things' ever made were carved from wood. As soon as early humans learned how to make stone tools, they used these to alter the other materials around them. Stone tools allowed our ancestors to chop trees, split them into planks, plane their surfaces and whittle small sections into points or other shapes.

As we saw from WOODWORKING (pages 174-177), the earliest wooden objects were probably spears or digging sticks, carved to a point with sharp stone tools. The earliest carved wooden object uncovered to date is known as the Clacton Spear.

It's a 400,000-year-old thing of beauty – a ruler-long, tapered length of yew, patiently carved into a sharp point at one end – and was found just before the First World War on the foreshore at the English seaside resort Clacton-on-Sea. The man who picked it up thought it was an antler at first, its shape was so smooth and pointed, and for decades sceptics wouldn't entertain the idea that very early humans (probably the predecessor of both Neanderthals and modern humans, *Homo heidelbergensis*) could make something so sophisticated as a spear. The argument was finally settled when, in the late 1990s, a set of eight similar, 330,000-year-old spears turned up in a German open-cast mine, along with 10,000 animal bones from wild horses, bison and red deer that had been hunted, killed and eaten.

The oldest wooden carved statue is the Shigir Idol, a 3-metre-tall, totem pole-like structure discovered in a peat bog in the Ural Mountains. It's impressive not only for its age – at 11,000 years old, it's more than twice as old as Egypt's Great Pyramid or England's Stonehenge – but also for its skilled woodcarving. Research on the Shigir Idol has revealed that, to create the sculpture, the carver(s) would have had to use at least three different stone chisels of different sizes and 'sandpapered' the larch timber surface with a fine-grained abrasive. Even more fascinating, to create the statue's various faces, the carver used sharpened beaver teeth, still held in place in the jaw bone. Beaver teeth aside, many of the modern woodcarver's tools would look familiar to the ancient craftsperson. Chisels, gouges, skews, V-parting tools, wooden mallets and carving knives: this select group of tools can perform a huge range of tasks.

SPOON CARVING

One of the most surprising success stories in recent years has been the phenomenal interest in spoon carving. Perhaps it's the fact that it's a craft you can pick up in a few hours (although it takes years to master) or that the end result is tactile and functional, spoon carving has taken on a cult craft status. There's something deeply satisfying about acquiring a new skill, especially one that delivers an instant object – something that you can take home in your pocket and use on a daily basis.

Spoon carving is also a craft that's taken urban dwellers by storm, perhaps because it's so accessible. There are now numerous workshops and courses that teach the techniques, using traditional tools and green, unseasoned wood. Thanks to the efforts of carvers such as Robin Wood and Barnaby Carder aka Barn the Spoon, a whole new generation of people is becoming interested in working with wood. There's even an annual Spoonfest in the UK and The Spoon Gathering in the US, both celebrations of the skills, tools and techniques of traditional spoon carving.

‖‖

DID YOU KNOW?

The word 'spoon' comes from the Old English *spōn*, and the even earlier Proto-Indo-European speh meaning 'chip, shaving or length of wood'.

‖‖

WOODTURNING

Most woodwork involves clamping or holding a piece of timber in place, and moving a cutting tool around the wood to shape it. Whether it's carving a sculpture or sawing a plank, the wood stays static and the tool moves. In woodturning, it's the opposite. The wood rotates at high speed and the cutting tool stays relatively still, shaving off tiny slivers of wood to create a shape with rotational symmetry, such as a bowl, spindle or goblet. The turner uses a tool called a lathe – a machine that shapes the wood by rotating it rapidly along its axis – while he or she presses a cutting tool against it.

It's an ancient technique, although historians don't know an awful lot about its origins. The earliest example is a flat wooden dish found in a grave to the north of Athens dating to 1400–1100 B.C., but by the 7th and 6th centuries B.C. carefully turned wooden platters, boxes, bowls and dishes turn up across north Italy, Turkey, Crimea and Germany.

These early pieces were turned on a strap lathe, which needed two people to operate. One person (usually an apprentice or young assistant) had to continuously pull a length of cord back and forward, which rotated the lathe, while the wood turner could work on the spinning wood. Turning wood by this method was hard work, especially for the cord 'puller', and necessitated two sets of wages. One solution was the bow lathe, a machine similar to the strap lathe except that the rotation was powered by the reciprocating backwards and forwards motion of a bow. The turner could hold the bow in one hand and the cutting tool in the other, removing the need for an assistant. The downside of this technique was that the bow lathe wasn't as powerful as the strap lathe and it was tricky to steady the cutting tool with just one hand; some deft woodturners took to using their foot to support the cutting tool. There are some fantastic images in a 13th-century book, *Libro de los Juegos* (*Book of Games*), showing two men turning wooden backgammon and chess pieces on a bow lathe using their feet.

A breakthrough came with the invention of the pole lathe. The crucial difference was the addition of a treadle, which the woodturner could press with his foot to make the lathe rotate. (The word 'pole' refers to the long bendy stick that's used as a return-spring for the treadle.) Not only did this free up both hands, it also meant the turner could stand up to work – both strap and bow lathes required the crafter to sit on the floor – giving them more control over the pace and power of the cutting.

Interestingly, the development of different kinds of lathes doesn't happen in a linear way across the world. Even during the middle of the 20th century, the strap lathe was still in use in Ethiopia and the bow lathe in Egypt. Equally, the pole lathe didn't make much of a mark on Europe until the 13th century and yet we know, from archaeological evidence, that the Vikings were already skilled pole lathe turners in the 10th century.

Evidence from Yorvik, the Viking name for York, tells us more. The road name 'Coppergate', for example, comes not from any metallurgical association but from the Old Norse for 'street of the cup-makers'. There, archaeologists dug up hundreds of wood 'cores', the tell-tale debris that's left over from turning cups and bowls on a pole lathe. The woodturners of Coppergate were producing wooden cups and bowls on an impressively commercial scale, supplying beautifully crafted tableware for both the townsfolk of Viking York and its surrounding hinterland (also see NÅLEBINDING, pages 108–113).

FURNITURE MAKING

People have found themselves things to sit upon and sleep on, to eat things from and to store things in since pre-history. You can imagine the evolutionary process, from first finding a useful flat surface in your environment to eventually making one yourself from whatever material was to hand. In essence, that's the history of furniture making.

To look a bit more closely; a distinct craft of making jointed furniture (mainly from wood) was well established by the time of the pharaohs in Egypt (see WOODWORKING, pages 174–177) and has continued to evolve since then. In fact, it's still evolving. One of the interesting threads in that story is the growing gap between, on the one hand, making everyday affordable objects close to where they would be used and on the other, making objects of conspicuously high quality using rare and expensive materials and of a distinct style. Only the very wealthiest could afford the latter. At one end of the scale, it's mainly about utility; about how to make things that do the job, are tough enough to withstand the demands of life and yet are affordable. At the other, usefulness is a consideration but the objects also had to be a symbol of the taste and wealth of their owner.

It's an important tension to think about, because it underpins our decisions about whose work and ideas deserve to be studied. It has a direct bearing on how we think about where craft furniture making fits now.

Take the everyday end first. There has been a continuous tradition of making chairs, tables, beds and cupboards in local workshops since before medieval times. A supply chain evolved from felling and preparing timber, through to delivering the finished item. In the case of chairs, a few men would be the entire chain. A bodger turned legs from timber as near as possible to where the trees grew, a benchman made the seats and back splats, then a framer put it all together to make a chair.

Designs were like local dialects. They were distinctive and evolved. You can tell which part of England a Windsor chair hails from, for example, by how the legs are braced apart. A man making a simple planked bedding chest would do it in the same way his father did, although he might make something special if the order had come from the bishop, not least as an expression of his own faith. So design, in vernacular furniture, was a mixture of tradition, local timber, the experience of what had worked before, and a conversation with whoever had ordered the item. Decoration would be simply applied and locally distinctive.

In total contrast, Europe in the 18th century saw a great flowering of furniture designers. In Britain, Chippendale, Hepplewhite and Sheraton produced books of designs aimed at wealthy British people. Gillow in Lancaster did the same and produced work, mainly in mahogany, much of which survives in high-status houses. Their designs were elegant, sometimes highly decorated and involved in their quality and had significant costs of production. Fashion rippled around the furniture world – from Rococo to Classical, Gothic to Regency, Victorian to Arts and Crafts and then Art Nouveau and Modernism, much influenced by foreign styles, new timbers and counter-waves of nostalgia. As ever, makers producing work for the less wealthy tried to reflect the current fashions, with varying degrees of quality.

In late 19th-century England, William Morris shook up the worlds of furniture, interior decoration, PRINTING and architecture, not to mention the politics of labour and production. In a new world of mechanised production, Morris wanted work to recapture the dignity of individual craftmanship. He saw men making honest items for sale that would reflect their skill and choices. Morris intensely disliked over-ornate objects of any kind; his 'new craftsmen' would make much simpler,

cleaner items from durable materials. His philosophy affected people around him profoundly. Ernest Gimson put Morris's thoughts into practice in Edwardian England by setting up a furniture workshop in rural Gloucestershire. He taught local people to make simple furniture out of local hardwood. Other makers came to the Cotswolds and craft workshops flourished: PRINTING, SMITHING, EMBROIDERY, chairmaking and TEXTILES. Most discovered that the resulting objects of great beauty came with prices that put them well beyond the pockets of working people. But in these brave early 20th-century attempts at work with honesty and dignity may lie the beginnings of our enduring enthusiasm for craft furniture.

In the 20th century, the spirit of craftsmanship flourished. Furniture makers' materials changed to include metal, advanced plywoods, fabrics and plastics. Designers on all continents fused industrial techniques and materials to produce radically new styles, some for mass production, some to be made in specialist workshops; certain names became renowned - the Bauhaus School in Germany, Charles and Ray Eames in the US, the Scandinavian designer Arne Jacobsen and Vico Magistretti in Italy.

Today, craft furniture making is very healthy, especially in the UK and the US, thanks in part to the work of two men. Alan Peters (who died in 2009) designed and made beautiful furniture and was a direct link to William Morris through his apprenticeship to the Cotswold maker, Edward Barnsley. His lasting impact will be through his writing of the standard handbooks for furniture makers. His memory is also celebrated with an Annual Award For Excellence in Furniture Design and Making. John Makepeace, himself a highly skilled designer and maker, set up the hugely influential Parnham College in the UK. Its former students include some of our greatest contemporary makers, including David Linley, Rod and Alison Wales and Isabelle Moore. Makepeace was a strong advocate for furniture design and had an early hand in the British Crafts Council.

Young furniture makers are also taking the craft scene by storm. People such as Edward Johnson, who finished college in 2006 and set up his workshop, designs and makes beautiful, striking furniture which makes completely fresh use of curve-formed plywood and veneer. Training opportunities are also in healthy supply, with a strong mixture of courses in local colleges and regional universities. Many makers run shorter courses in their own

studios and successful workshops offer apprenticeships. There is also strong national support, in the UK for example, from the Crafts Council, the Design Council and the regional programmes to support arts and business development.

The work of a furniture maker is an interesting blend of business and making. Most furniture makers work in response to specific requests. The client asks for a piece (usually having bought something from this maker before or having seen work at an exhibition). Client and maker meet, talk about what the piece is expected to do, where it is to go and about materials and finishes. For makers, fixing the price is vital but can be extraordinarily difficult; it's often a key issue in training.

With a contract agreed and deposit paid, the maker chooses the timber, sources the fittings and begins the process of converting rough seasoned wood into the item that has been chosen. It's often a solo process. Initially it's likely to involve substantial machining to produce dimensioned timber but then the handwork begins. Key stages, like cutting joints will either be done by hand or, more likely now, by basic machinery. Final assembly and finishing will involve hours of handwork. As in all craft work, the human possibility of mistakes and the variability of timber make it, in David Pye's words 'The Workmanship of Risk'; it's the defining characteristic of handwork, the realisation that, after hours of work, an item can be ruined by a moment's loss of concentration.

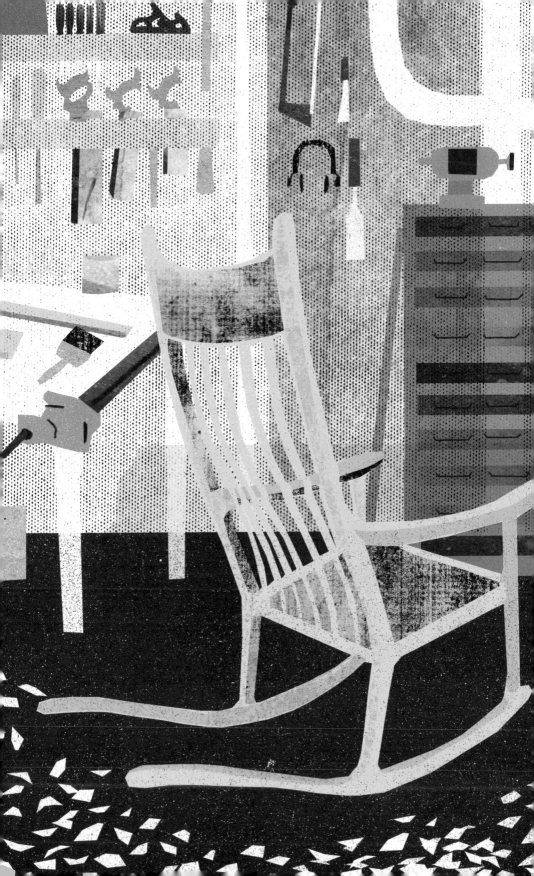

WHEELWRIGHTING

Wheelwrighting is a craft that's been around for thousands of years. Around 5000 B.C., the first solid wood wheels began to appear, but it's not until 3000 years later that anyone thought to create a lighter, spoked version. Iron Age tribes were masters of their art and created chariot wheels not dissimilar to those still made and repaired by wheelwrights today. The design is straightforward but takes skill to execute. A wooden hub (called a nave), into which spokes are fitted, is then surrounded with sections of curved timber, known as felloes (pronounced fellies), to create the body of the wheel. The wheel is then finished with a one-piece metal rim – a process known as 'tyring'.

A large part of the craft is knowing the materials; just in one wheel, for example, you traditionally find three types of wood – elm, ash and oak. Elm makes the hub or nave of the wheel, its interwoven grain making it resistant to splitting; ash creates the felloes – a flexible, springy timber, it's a natural shock absorber; and oak forms the spokes, a wood renowned for its strength, that doesn't bend or flex under pressure. Part of a wheelwright's skill is being able to 'read' the timber, and select the right sections for the task in hand.

Most wheelwrights working today take on a variety of jobs to keep them afloat, from cartwheels and carriages, wooden classic car wheels and repairs to gypsy caravans, windmills and shepherds' huts. Such a varied portfolio isn't unusual. Up until the First World War, most villages had their own wheelwright – when not making and repairing wheels, they would turn their hands to other timber projects such as hurdles, tool handles, gates, house repairs, even coffin making. Some wheelwrights worked alongside BLACKSMITHS (pages 212–219), others combined the two skills, but with the rise of motorised transport demand for the craft began to wane. By the 1960s, wheelwrighting was in trouble; by 2000, it had nearly disappeared.

Thanks to the quiet determination of remaining wheelwrights, such as Douglas Andrews in the UK and Mike Hendrickson in Australia, with the support of agencies such as the Wheelwrights' Livery Company and the Worshipful Company of Wheelwrights, who provide funding for apprenticeships, the craft has thankfully returned to a sustainable position.

COOPERING

Anyone brought up on *Asterix* – the adventures that follow a village of Gauls as they resist Caesar's Imperial occupation – will know that the comic books conjure up an image of an Iron Age society that enjoyed nothing more than eating wild boar, getting into punch-ups with Roman soldiers and drinking vast quantities of alcohol. While Asterix was clearly a cheerful exaggeration, there's a grain of truth in this historical stereotype. It seems the Gauls loved drinking; so much so, in fact, the historian Diodorus of Sicily, writing in the 1st century B.C., described them as 'exceedingly addicted to the use of wine', while another contemporary observer, Strabo, wrote with astonishment of Gauls bulk buying wine from northern Italy and storing it in their own casks, often with huge capacities of well over 1,000 litres.

The Gauls may not have invented wooden barrels – the oldest example comes from a drawing on the Egyptian tomb of Hesi-Re (circa 2600 B.C.) and shows a wooden cask made from planks held together with bentwood hoops – but what they did do was develop and refine the technique of coopering to create barrels capable of the large-scale transport and storage of goods. The reasons why aren't clear. Perhaps the availability of high-quality local timber played its part, or the fact that the Gauls were skilled wood and metalworkers. Whatever the driving force, it's thanks to the Gauls' passion for plonk that the wooden barrel became such a ubiquitous and popular way of transporting goods. Even the Romans eventually ditched their beloved clay amphorae in favour of the humble wooden barrel.

Barrels, when you think about it, are an ingenious shape. The bulging waist (called a bilge) of a barrel allows it to be rolled along and also spun around, making it highly manoeuvrable. Wooden barrels are also the perfect vehicle for storing wine: when stacked horizontally, a barrel's shape allows you to draw off wine without getting any of the sediment that has collected at the bottom; wood breathes, allowing the contents of the barrel to mature over time; and the type of wood used to make a barrel can impart flavour and colour into wine – oak, pine, eucalyptus and chestnut being just a handful of species used over the centuries. As a method of transporting goods, they're virtually peerless. Not only are wooden barrels robust and re-usable, they can also hold liquids under pressure, float on water, and resist enormous loads under compression.

Whether the craft of coopering developed from other practices that involved similar materials and skills, such as boat building or BASKET WEAVING (pages 160–163), is difficult to say. As with all perishable wooden objects, the archaeology is scant. There are few surviving early examples – the occasional barrel stave (curved piece of timber) turns up on waterlogged excavations now and again – and, as we already know, there are etymological links between words such as trug, trough, vessel and boat (see TRUGMAKING, pages 166–167) that suggest a shared craft ancestry.

|||||||||||||||||||||||||||||||||||||||||||||||||||||||||||||||||||

DID YOU KNOW?

A 'barrel' is actually a specific quantity in brewing – in the UK it's 36 imperial gallons. You also get pins, firkins and kilderkins, which are smaller than barrels, and puncheons, tuns, hogsheads and butts, which are larger.

|||||||||||||||||||||||||||||||||||||||||||||||||||||||||||||||||||

What's clear, however, is just how skilled the craft of coopering is. The precision and craftsmanship needed to create a container that's watertight are only learned through years of apprenticeship and refinement. From sourcing the right timber and seasoning it, to coercing the staves into curves and charring the interior of the finished barrel (a process called toasting), many of the stages in coopering have a profound impact on the contents of the barrel. It's often said that the cooper's craft is just as important as the brewer's when it comes to finished product.

The introduction of metal casks in the middle of the 20th century struck a severe blow to the craft but thanks to the continued use of wooden barrels by the wine industry, along with distilleries and microbreweries, a handful of coopers continue the craft. In Scotland, there are around 200 coopers still producing barrels for the whisky industry, but in England the craft is being kept alive by one man alone – master cooper Alastair Simms – who still crafts casks, vats and barrels by hand using traditional methods.

TIMBER FRAMING

We often imagine Roman cities to be built from stone. Yet when Queen Boudicca and her bloodthirsty rebel army stormed London in A.D. 60, it was filled with thatched wooden houses and workshops, the perfect structures for setting fire to. In fact, so complete was Boudicca's destruction of Roman *Londinium* that dig down almost anywhere within the old boundaries of the city and you can still clearly see the thin blanket of ash and burnt timber left behind.

Timber-framed houses have, in fact, been around for thousands of years. We only have to look to the 11,000-year-old remains of a wooden house at Star Carr in Yorkshire (see THATCHING, pages 170–173) to understand its ancient heritage. Anywhere that had access to plentiful deciduous forests, from Japan to Denmark, England to China, could exploit the potential of timber as a tough, durable and readily available building material.

Early housebuilders drove the timber posts of their constructions directly into the soil, with much of the strength of the building being derived from how firmly it was anchored in the ground. Posts rot when in contact with earth, however, and so a major development in timber framing came when crafters worked out how to build a timber

||||||||||||||||||||||||||||||||||||||||||||||||||||||||||||||||||||

DID YOU KNOW?

Cruck framed houses can look, on the inside, like upturned ships. People often mistakenly assume that the huge, curved timbers for these buildings were reclaimed from dismantled boats. They weren't – it's just an ancient way of creating walls and a roof using pairs of curved timbers braced together.

||||||||||||||||||||||||||||||||||||||||||||||||||||||||||||||||||||

frame that could sit above ground and get its strength from the connections (such as mortice-and-tenon joints) made between the lengths of timber instead.

One of the most appealing traits of timber-framed buildings is their variety. Different communities across the world have used the same material in varying ways, producing their own, local interpretations. Access to timber has also influenced the type of building produced: in the UK, for example, in densely forested counties such as Cheshire, Shropshire and Wiltshire, there was and still is a profusion of wooden buildings, with timber framing remaining a popular building technique well into the 18th century. In stone-rich upland areas, such as the Yorkshire Dales and North York Moors, timber frames were often used in conjunction with stone walls, while in Cornwall, a county with few trees suitable for timber construction, timber-framed buildings are scarce. The construction varies, too. As a broad rule, cruck-framed houses (with curved timbers like an upturned boat) are found across northern, western and midland England, but rarely in

East Anglia and the southeast. Box frames, on the other hand, where timbers are joined together to form a cube and infilled with panels of wattle and daub, and later brick, are more widespread.

The craft of timber framing is more than simply building with wood. People who still make traditional timber frames will tell you that the work is multifaceted: the design stage, the understanding of structure and loads, the marking out of the timber, the physicality needed to cut the joints and assemble the frame. A key skill, for example, is the crafter's ability to 'read' a piece of timber and understand how its natural curves and innate strength can be used to their best effect. Many of the techniques haven't changed since the Middle Ages - using cruck frames or hammerbeam roofs - and the hand tools would also be familiar to a medieval carpenter - the adze, the draw knife and the carpenter's axe.

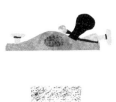

LIME PLASTERING

Scientists recently discovered an extraordinary fact about the Great Wall of China; that workers who built this ancient wonder of the world during the Ming Dynasty stuck the building blocks together with a mixture of sticky rice flour and lime mortar. The resulting 'natural' cement was so strong that it's still intact more than 600 years later. In fact, most of history's greatest brick and stone buildings were held together, not with modern cement (which wasn't invented until the 1820s), but with lime. The Egyptians were plastering their pyramids with lime as long as 6000 years ago, while the Romans developed a version of lime, called hydraulic lime, that could harden even under water.

|||||||||||||||||||||||||||||||||||||||||||||||||||||||||||||||

DID YOU KNOW?

The Roman recipe for hydraulic lime has a tougher molecular structure than modern cement. Made from a mix of volcanic ash and lime, and impervious to the corrosive effects of salt water, this Roman building material is the reason so many ancient port buildings, aqueducts and jetties have survived the last two thousand years.

|||||||||||||||||||||||||||||||||||||||||||||||||||||||||||||||

Lime is made by heating limestone until it becomes a powdery substance called 'quicklime' or calcium oxide. Water is then added to the quicklime to make a flexible putty that can be mixed with other ingredients such as sand, horse hair or gypsum to make everything from mortar to render, plaster to pointing and paints. It's a wonderful material. Old buildings tend to move (they often have shallow foundations or are made from materials, such as wood and handmade brick, that expand and contract with changes in the weather). Unlike cement, lime can accommodate these movements – in fact, small cracks in lime can even heal themselves, a process called autogenous healing. Lime also absorbs condensation and allows damp to evaporate, enabling buildings to 'breathe' and shed water.

Modern cement and old buildings don't go together. Many an old house and barn have been ruined, often unintentionally, by builders using hard cement instead of lime. Few trades, outside conservation circles, are comfortable using traditional lime – the mixes, techniques and drying times are very different from cement – but thankfully a growing number of craftspeople, eco-builders and restoration specialists are incorporating lime into their projects.

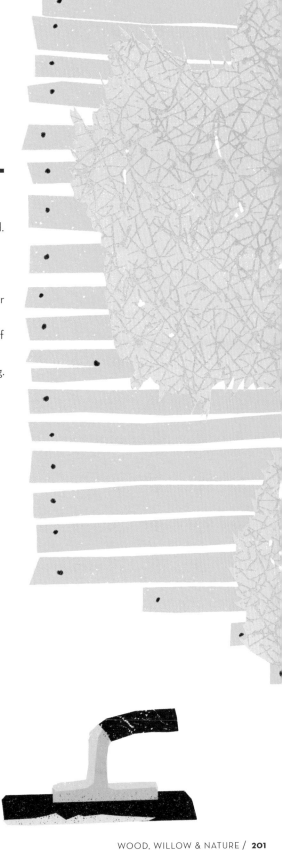

PLASTERWORK & PARGETTING

Conservation plasterers are also in demand.
Historic buildings often need sections
of ornamental lime plasterwork, such as
cornicing or stucco, repairing or replacing.
Different counties in England also have their
own limework techniques. Suffolk, Essex
and Norfolk have the vernacular tradition of
pargetting (also spelled 'pargeting'), a form
of highly decorative external lime plastering.
The word pargetting comes from 'parge',
the original name for the plasterers' mix
of sand, lime and hair. Historically, many
ingredients have been used in parge mixes,
many of which were incorporated to affect
drying times or change the consistency or
colour of the mix, and include urine, tallow,
blood, soot, manure and even cheese.

METAL

GOLDSMITHING

It's interesting that we still divide the history of human development into three crude stages: the Stone Age, the Bronze Age and the Iron Age. Metal, and its use by humans, has been seen as the defining characteristic of a society's evolution and, in particular, the use of metals for tools and weapons. It's telling that there's no 'Cotton Age', for example, or 'Literacy Age'.

Mankind's relationship with metal has always been a special one. Our earliest experiences of any metals would have been those that occurred naturally, in a pure form on the earth's surface, and caught our eye with their dazzling difference. It's not difficult to imagine one of our prehistoric ancestors wading through a shallow river bed, her gaze suddenly captured by the glint of a tiny gold nugget or clump of pure copper. Such attention-grabbing treasures would have surely been prized for their aesthetic value, if nothing else; some of the more adventurous among the group may have experimented to see what happened when the metal nugget was hammered with a stone tool, soon discovering that these shiny lumps were also malleable and easy to work into different shapes. Other groups might have taken it a step further – heating the metal in an open fire – and discovering that this precious new material could be melted and cast into useful shapes.

The timeline of metallurgy can be confusing. Different cultures discovered various metals and techniques at different times. But what's clear is that, since the Late Neolithic period, people have been playing around with copper and gold, often with striking results. The Native Americans, for example, have been using copper for small tools for around 5,000 years, while Europe's Ötzi the Ice Man (see FUR & LEATHER, pages 78–81) was found with a copper axe dating to a similar age. What's more, the axe was made not from locally sourced deposits, but copper from southern Tuscany. The implications for this are huge. As long as 5000 years ago, there were extensive trade links between the Stone Age people of central Italy and those 300 miles away in the southern Alps.

Anyone experimenting with these 'native metals' would have soon realised that their attractive colour and soft workability made them ideal for jewellery. One of the most spectacular archaeological hauls of all time comes from this early period of metalwork. In the early 1970s, in Bulgaria, a young workman was digging the foundations for a new canning factory just outside the city of Varna. On discovering a few unusual artefacts in the ground, he took them home in a shoe box. After a few days, he contacted a local archaeologist.

The ensuing excavation uncovered almost 300 graves, dating to around 4600–4200 B.C. Each grave was different and filled with treasures, but the most glittering of all was Grave No. 43, belonging to a man in his forties. His burial site was an embarrassment of gold riches: rings, necklaces, beads, decorations for a bow, and even a gold penis sheath, all in all weighing a total of 1.5 kg. In fact, this single grave contained more gold than all of the

||||||||||||||||||||||||||||||||||||||||||||||||||||||||||||||||||||

DID YOU KNOW?

An Italian archeologist was rifling through Vatican archives when he discovered a 17th-century letter from a missionary called Andreas Lopez. In it, Lopez described 'Paititi', an Incan city stuffed full of exquisite gold artefacts and jewellery. Archaeologists and treasure hunters have searched for this lost city of gold ever since, hoping to find the hoard for themselves. The search still continues but isn't without its dangers – in 1971 an expedition of French and American explorers went into the jungle and never came out. In 1997, a Norwegian team made the same attempt and, too, failed to return.

||||||||||||||||||||||||||||||||||||||||||||||||||||||||||||||||||||

other archaeological sites from that period put together. The grave also contained a large number of copper artefacts, including an axe, chisel, claw hammer and awl.

Most of history's jaw-dropping and popular archaeological finds belong to the craft of goldsmithing. The craft captures the imagination; the fine workmanship, combined with the rarity and value of gold, never fail to make headlines. From Anglo-Saxon Sutton Hoo to the priceless Panagyurishte treasure (which included 6 kg of solid gold carved into elaborate drinking horns, decanters and dishes) of Bulgaria, the craft of goldsmithing reached a level of high sophistication across the globe thousands of years ago. Goldsmiths working today would recognise many of the methods and tools of the ancient goldsmith, a point beautifully demonstrated by the treasures plundered from Ancient Egyptian tombs.

Egypt was rich in gold. The earliest surviving artefacts date to the fourth millennium B.C. – mostly small beads and other simple pieces of jewellery – but soon the dynastic goldsmiths were producing work of staggering technical accomplishment. Egyptian goldsmiths could make delicate gold wire, cast gold into solid objects and even hammer gold leaf to less than a hair's breadth (0.005mm). In fact, many of the treasures of Egypt are created from hammered sheets of gold, which are then applied as a veneer to other materials, formed into shapes, or fixed together with small gold rivets. These thicker gold sheets were also often embossed or engraved. One of the wives of Thutmose III, for example, was buried with flip-flops made from a hammered gold sheet with scored and stamped decoration on the sole. Too fragile to have ever been worn, these ancient sandals were instead designed to be footwear fit for the afterlife.

These Ancient Egyptian crafters also knew techniques such as inlaying, cloisonné, granulation, and even developed an early form of soldering. In fact, across the globe, and throughout the millennia, the craft of the goldsmith has proved to be one of the most astounding and advanced of all human endeavours – from the Moche culture of northern Peru to the Scythian nomads of southern Russia, the ancient city of Troy to Britain's Stonehenge, our love of all things shiny pushed the craft to its very limits.

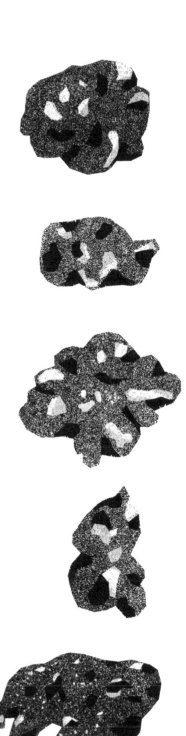

BRONZESMITHING

Native metals, such as gold and copper, may have formed brilliantly lustrous jewellery and decorative objects, but they didn't make particularly strong tools and weapons. Gold and copper are both soft in their pure forms. Smelted copper is also very malleable to start off with and, if you work it too much, it gradually hardens and becomes brittle. Tricky, if you want to make axe heads and knives that won't bend or crack at the first sign of action.

If you melt copper, however, and mix it with another material, you can create an alloy that is tougher and more durable than copper alone. To begin with, people mixed arsenic with copper, to produce an alloy called arsenic bronze, also known as 'dirty copper'. We find examples of arsenic bronze artefacts in places such as Iran, Iraq and Syria from as far back as the 5th century B.C. But there's one fundamental problem with arsenic bronze; arsenic fumes are highly poisonous (see POISONOUS CRAFTS, pages 226–227). One well-known side effect of long-term arsenic poisoning is nerve damage and lameness. It's interesting that the Greek god of metalworking, Hephaestus, is often described as walking with a limp or using a cane.

Despite its toxicity, arsenic bronze continued to be used throughout the Middle East, Europe and China for the next 2000 years. Even Ötzi – our frozen friend from the Alps – had high levels of copper and arsenic particles in samples of his hair, leading archaeologists to conclude that he probably smelted dirty copper during his lifetime.

Sometime towards the end of the 3rd millennium, it was widely discovered that the addition of tin, instead of arsenic, produced a superior alloy, known as tin bronze. Unlike its toxic predecessor, tin bronze was actually easier to produce and to cast into shapes; it heralded the period known as the Bronze Age. Such was the popularity of the material that both men and women in many societies would have owned and used a number of bronze objects. Danish Bronze Age burials, for example, show that women often wore large bronze belt ornaments, while men were buried with razors and swords. Both men and women wore bronze jewellery, such as clothes pins, arm bands and torcs (stiff necklaces), and would carry a bronze dagger. Every household would also have at least one bronze axe, for everyday jobs such as chopping wood and carpentry.

Such was the ubiquity and demand for bronze objects that the role of the bronzesmith was an important one.

Evidence suggests that smiths may have
been itinerant – travelling from village
to village, like door-to-door salesmen –
carrying samples of the kinds of things they
could make. If welcomed in, a smith might
stay a while, setting up a small temporary
workshop and cast products to order.
There's even a theory that he would recycle
a village's old bronze tools and weapons,
melting them down and creating newer,
more fashionable items in their place.

From ethnographic studies of more recent,
non-ferrous, smiths in places such as
West Africa and India, it's clear that the
craft is one that's hugely respected but
also, at times, feared. Smiths are often
viewed as powerful, magical crafters, who
have mastered the elements and possess
'powers' that allow them to transform
one object into another. 'The art of
creating tools is essentially superhuman,'
as one historian, Eliade, noted, 'either
divine or demoniac (for the smith also
forges murderous weapons).' Similarly,
in Mycenaean Greece, the job of the
bronzesmith was a high-ranking, privileged
role, often handed down through the family.
Because he made bronze items for religious
ceremonies, the smith had to be specially
consecrated and was often given assistants
or servants to help with his 'divine' work.

Until recently, it was thought that ancient
smithing was always a man's job. Then,
in Austria, a grave was uncovered that
changed everything.

In it lay a mature female, aged between 45 and 60, interred with the tools of her metalwork trade. In legend, smiths have also been women. In Ireland, for example, the divine smith is Brigit, goddess of fire and metalworking. (Incidentally, the name 'Britain' comes from the Brigantes, the ancient Celtic tribe who worshipped Brigit).

||||||||||||||||||||||||||||||||||||||||||||||||||||||||||||||||

DID YOU KNOW?

The remains of human bones have appeared repeatedly in Bronze Age smith's furnaces, particularly in Scandinavia. Quite why they are there is a mystery, but one theory is that human bones were useful fuel for achieving the very high temperatures needed for smelting. Whether these bones belonged to sacrificial victims or simply willing 'donors' has never been established.

||||||||||||||||||||||||||||||||||||||||||||||||||||||||||||||||

BLACKSMITHING

Ancient cultures often looked to the stars for divine inspiration. For once, their prayers were answered because the earliest iron ever found fell, quite literally, from the sky. Meteoric iron – the iron that plummets to earth during meteor showers – provided our prehistoric ancestors with a rare but useful source of metal. Small lumps would be found, where they'd fallen, and because they had few impurities could be hammered into shapes without needing to be heated.

The oldest known iron artefacts are made from this out-of-this-world metal and include a handful of Egyptian small beads dated to 3200 B.C. and an iron dagger found in Tutankhamun's tomb. In fact, archaeologists had long been puzzled by iron objects that turned up on sites much older than the invention of iron smelting technology. Only when these objects were later analysed did it become clear that they were made from meteoric iron, which contains a tell-tale high percentage of nickel. From a precious Syrian iron pendant dating to 2300 B.C. to Chinese iron artefacts 3400 years old from the Shang dynasty, it turns out that all of these early iron treasures came from cosmic sources.

Meteoric iron has landed across the globe for thousands of years and has been a valuable and useful resource for many cultures, especially those who didn't have access to iron smelting or who were isolated from the exchange of ideas and technology. So precious were these sources of 'space metal' that many societies venerated meteors and meteoric iron as gifts from the gods. Celestial metal was often attributed with supernatural origins and, therefore, supernatural power. Writing in 1975, one commentator recorded the experiences of a group of Native Americans Indians and their veneration of a vast, 14-tonne iron meteorite that landed in Willamette, Oregon:

'One Indian was Susap, a 70-year-old Klickitat, who testified that he had seen the meteorite as a child and had been told by Wochimo, Chief of the Clackamas, that the Indians washed their faces in the water collected at the basins of the meteorite, and that their young warriors dipped their arrows in the water before engaging in battle with neighbouring tribes.'
(Buchanan, 1975)

The issue with meteoric iron and other native metals, such as gold, is that although they are pure and easily hammered into shapes, they're incredibly rare. It was no accident that most of the objects made with these metals were either destined for high-ranking individuals or connected to some kind of important ritual. As the name suggests, terrestrial iron – the ubiquitous metal that makes everything from bridges to bath tubs – comes from a very different source and requires a huge amount of processing before it can be crafted into useful objects.

Terrestrial iron comes from sedimentary rocks. It's one of the most abundant elements in the Earth's crust but, unlike meteoric iron, is found as 'iron ore'. This messy mix of iron, oxygen and other impurities make it useless without processing. To extract iron from iron ore you need to heat it up. The earliest attempts at this used small furnaces fuelled by charcoal, which got just hot enough to drive off the oxygen, leaving behind a spongy lump of almost pure iron called 'bloom'. The bloom could then be reheated in a fire and hammered into weapons, tools and other objects by a smith. This new material became known as 'wrought iron' (wrought is the ancient word for 'worked').

While people in the region now known as the Middle East had been experimenting with smelting iron ore since around 2000 B.C., it took another 800 years for the technology really to take hold, a point that marked the beginning of the Iron Age. Quite why it took so long to switch from bronze to iron is a question long debated by archaeologists, but at least two things may have come into play: the first reason is that bronze was actually a perfectly good material for tools and weapons and it would have only been supplanted once iron production had become sufficiently reliable and high-quality enough to replace it; the second reason may be linked to problems with supplies of tin, which were needed to make bronze. Around 1300 B.C., there were disruptions to trade routes that traditionally supplied metalworkers of the Middle East with tin, possibly forcing them to look elsewhere for materials. Whatever the reason, when iron technology took hold it spread swiftly and widely, reaching the Mediterranean and South Asia by the 12th century B.C., and British shores by 700 B.C. Interestingly, new evidence suggests that India may have developed its own iron smelting technology very early – and completely independently of the rest of the world – around 1800 B.C. Sub-Saharan Africa also developed iron metallurgy around 1000 B.C. It's still not known whether this technology crept in via the Mediterranean or sprung up independently.

The people who crafted iron using a furnace, anvil and hammer, became known as 'blacksmiths' – a word that first makes an appearance around the 13th century. From its earliest days to the Industrial Revolution, the blacksmith played a pivotal role in village life, often making a variety of tools, household goods, agricultural equipment,

horseshoes, weapons and armour, and doubling up as the local WHEELWRIGHT (pages 192–193) or farrier (someone who shoes horses). In medieval communities, the blacksmith held an important position; from the small rural community blacksmith making tools and horseshoes, to the castle blacksmith crafting defensive metalwork and weapons and armour for men-at-arms. Monks also trained as blacksmiths in their own monasteries, and in larger towns blacksmiths often belonged to guilds and held positions of local power.

With the rise of industry from the mid-1700s onwards, the blacksmith struggled to compete against mass-produced iron goods, shaped in factories, and cheaper cast iron. Many subsisted as farriers or, later, at the beginning of the 20th century found work creating architectural ironwork or in the new automobile industry and by the 1950s blacksmithing was all but an obsolete trade. And yet, as with many traditional crafts, blacksmithing wasn't down for long. The 1970s and 80s saw a resurgence of interest in self-sufficiency and rural crafts, and a boom in conservation architecture, all of which encouraged a new generation of crafters to try their hand at blacksmithing. Trailblazers such as Yorkshire's Chris Topp, now a market leader in heritage ironwork, reinvigorated the craft and proved there was a market for hand-forged, high-quality ironwork. Today, blacksmithing is more popular than ever – estimates suggest there are now more smiths than there were in the Middle Ages, making everything from bespoke garden decoration, railings and handrails to gates, knives and sculpture.

It's also a craft that's grabbed the attention of a younger demographic. Programmes such as the US TV show Forged in Fire, the explosion of ironwork courses, and the popularity of crafters such as YouTube sensation Alec Steele (who has over a million subscribers to date) have revealed that modern blacksmithing is not only a worthwhile craft in so many ways but also financially viable as a career and a surprisingly popular spectator sport.

DID YOU KNOW?

One of the oldest and most widespread fairy tales is the 'Smith and the Devil', which dates back to the Bronze Age. In it, a Smith makes a deal with the devil, but tricks him at the last moment. The myth is still found in countries as diverse as India and Scandinavia, suggesting a shared cultural heritage some 6000 years ago.

CAST METAL WORKING

One of the limitations of early iron production was that metalworkers simply couldn't get their furnaces hot enough to liquefy the iron, which allowed it to be poured into moulds (iron has a very high melting point compared to, say, gold or silver). Then, in the 6th century B.C., Chinese metalworkers in the southern state of Wu ingeniously worked out a way to get temperatures high enough to turn iron molten. Changes in furnace design, better clay walls, more efficient air flow, hotter fuel, adding phosphorus to the process to reduce iron's melting temperature – all of these 'tweaks' allowed the Chinese to create cast-iron objects centuries ahead of the rest of the world. But, while cast iron was cheaper and easier to turn into objects (compared to laboriously hammering wrought iron into shape), it wasn't a particularly robust material and was often too brittle to be used for swords or other striking implements. The earliest cast-iron objects were therefore utilitarian items – cauldrons, ploughshares and structural pillars, for example – or decorative pieces.

The range of cast-iron objects that crafters produced was extraordinary, especially in light of their absence elsewhere in the world at this time. The Field Museum of natural history in Chicago possesses a varied collection of Chinese cast-iron objects, dating as early as the Wanning

States period (475–221 B.C.). In this amazing collection we find statues, plaques and bells, which would have served a ceremonial or decorative function. But we also see a great number of agricultural tools, such as sickles and hoes, and everyday items, including saws, spearheads, braziers, oil lamps, bowls, cooking pans and even 'hub caps' for chariot wheels. The Chinese were either very good at keeping secrets or news travelled slowly as, incredibly, the production of cast iron in England took another thousand years to arrive around 1500.

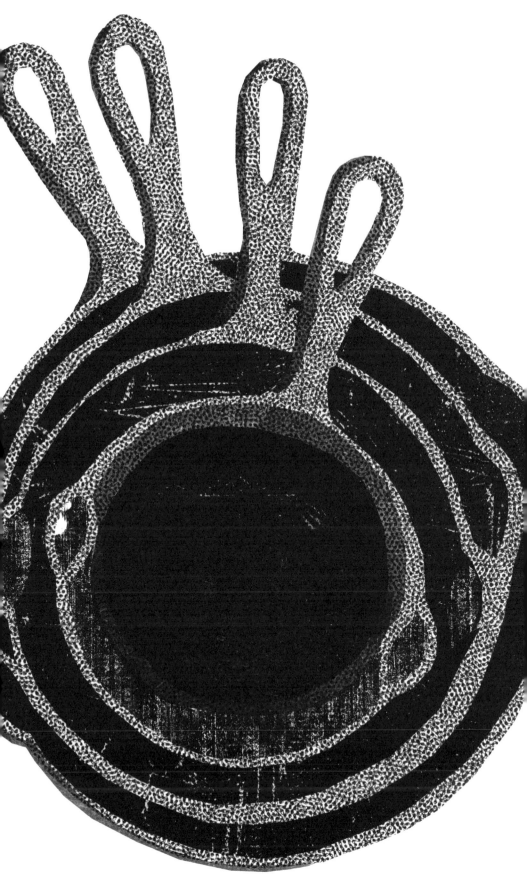

SWORDMAKING

As with all technology, there's always room for improvement and it wasn't long before metalworkers were tweaking with the smelting process to produce exciting new materials. As we know, early furnaces were fuelled by charcoal. At some stage, perhaps by accident, smiths noticed that if the iron was subjected to prolonged heat in the glowing charcoal it became harder and stronger; this is a process called carburisation, where iron absorbs the carbon from the charcoal and acquires a thin layer of carbon alloy or, as we know it, steel. This, and other trial-and-error methods such as overheating the metal and then quickly quenching it in water, would have resulted in a harder material, perfect

for knives, weapons and other cutting tools (the earliest quenched-steel object was a knife, found in Cyprus, dating to around 1100 B.C.).

Developments in metalworking often came in the form of weaponry. The success or failure of the blacksmith's craft could literally mean life or death in a battle. One of the most advanced skills demonstrated by Roman and Celtic blacksmiths in the 2nd century A.D. was producing pattern-welded blades. Iron that had acquired a thin layer of steel was repeatedly folded, or twisted, and hammered flat. In a process not dissimilar to making puff pastry, this endless manipulation had the effect of distributing fine laminations of steel throughout the material, creating rods of iron with unprecedented strength and durability. These iron rods could then be welded together and shaped into swords, which were polished or etched to reveal the beautiful complexity of the steel and iron structure. Hundreds of years later, this technique was inherited by the Vikings who were so proud of their creations they often signed them. The swords of one particular Viking workshop have been uncovered on excavations as far apart as Norway, France and Denmark. One even turned up on the bed of the River Thames. All bear the inscription 'Ingelrii', 'Ingelrd', 'Ingelrilt' or 'Ingerii me fecit' – 'Ingelrii made me'.

IIIIIIIIIIIIIIIIIIIIIIIIIIIIIIIIIIIIIIIIIIIIIIIIIIIIIIIIIIIIII

DID YOU KNOW?

Damascus steel had a reputation greater than any other. The steel, which became known to Europe when the Crusaders reached the Middle East, was said to be so sharp that it could split a feather in mid-air and yet retain a lethal toughness in battle. The original technique for making Damascus steel was lost over the centuries and, despite numerous attempts to recreate it, has never been authentically recreated.

IIIIIIIIIIIIIIIIIIIIIIIIIIIIIIIIIIIIIIIIIIIIIIIIIIIIIIIIIIIIII

KNIFE MAKING

Knife making is having a moment. Of all the different trades that come under the umbrella of BLACKSMITH (pages 214–221) work, knife making has captured the attention of both craft enthusiasts and the foodie movement. Connoisseurship of all kinds is cool and knives have become the thing for chefs and enthusiasts to commission, collect and compare. Not only is there an aesthetic element at play – bespoke knives can be things of extraordinary beauty and elegance – but the practical pleasure of using a well-made knife is incomparable to its mass-market equivalent. The makers are a gloriously diverse mix – from Grace Horne, Sheffield-based cutler (a city with its own 600 years of knife-making heritage), with her exquisitely designed scissors and knives, to Owen Bush who specialises in both Saxon and Viking knives, axes and swords. Social media-savvy knife makers also have huge, dedicated followers, from Britain's Ben Edmonds of Blok Knives and Texas-based Shawn Hatcher to South Africa's Jason Guthrie.

||||||||||||||||||||||||||||||||||||||||||||||||||||||||||||||||||

DID YOU KNOW?

The Santoku is the knife that is most commonly used in Japanese homes. Its name translates as 'three virtures' or 'strengths'.

||||||||||||||||||||||||||||||||||||||||||||||||||||||||||||||||||

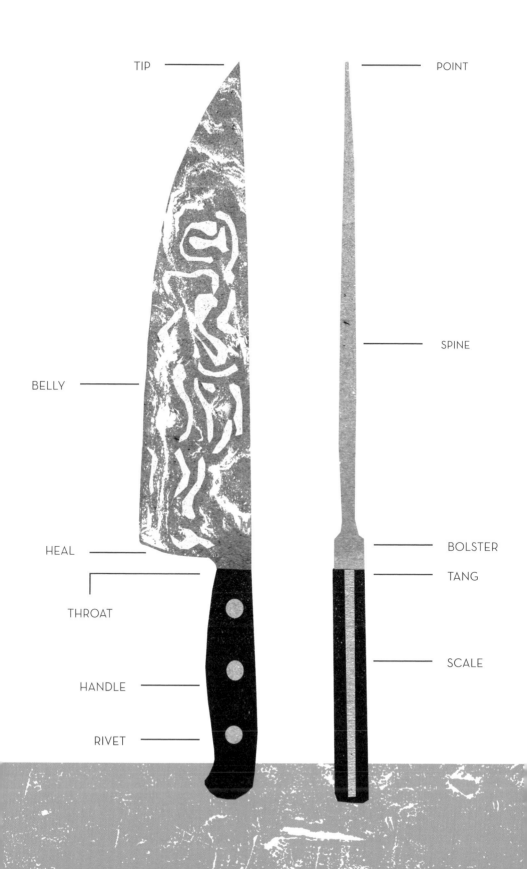

TIP

POINT

BELLY

SPINE

HEAL

BOLSTER

THROAT

TANG

HANDLE

SCALE

RIVET

POISONOUS CRAFTS

MERCURY

In the 1600s a process called 'carroting' was invented. It involved treating furry animal skins with a solution of mercuric nitrate (a compound of mercury) to turn them into top-quality felt for the production of hats. Mercury is highly toxic and both the solution and the vapours from the carroting process led to widespread mercury poisoning amongst hat makers and felt makers both in Europe and the US. Symptoms included speech problems, mental deterioration and tremors (known as 'hatters' shakes'). Despite the widespread knowledge that mercury caused serious health problems, the French and British craft industries didn't phase out the use of mercury until the end of the 19th century. Worse still, the US continued to use mercury until the Second World War.

LEAD

Lead has been used by crafters for thousands of years. We know that lead was being smelted as far back as 6000 B.C. and the Romans couldn't get enough of the stuff. They used it for everything from cosmetics to coins, sweetening wine to water pipes. (It's no coincidence that the word 'plumber' comes from the Latin for lead, *plumbum*.) Lead is useful stuff; it's soft and easy to work, making it the perfect metal for everything from jewellery to coins, lead pipes to bullets. It's also a transformative ingredient, making paint more durable and glass colourful and more sparkly. With the addition of lead, ceramic glazes could colour and waterproof a piece of pottery, while its ability to be melted at a low temperature made it ideal for making stained glass, architectural decoration, drinking vessels, printers' type and cast toys.

Crucially, lead is also deadly. Whether ingested or inhaled, lead is highly poisonous and potentially fatal. The symptoms are varied and unpleasant. Benjamin Franklin famously described painters and typesetters suffering with 'dry gripes' (stomach ache) and 'dangles' (wrist drop, a type of nerve palsy), while Charles Dickens met and wrote about victims of lead poisoning from Victorian London's notorious lead mills, who often suffered from seizures, mental deterioration and blindness. Amazingly, the Romans suspected lead might be poisonous. As early as A.D. 79, Pliny mentions lead poisoning amongst shipbuilders, but it took another 2000 years for clinicians to officially recognise the condition.

ARSENIC

Victorian Britain was slowly poisoning itself to death. Thanks, in large part, to one pigment: 'arsenic green'. First stumbled upon in the late 1700s and then perfected in 1814 by German industrialist, Wilhelm Sattler, this bold new green colour – derived from arsenic – was enthusiastically taken up by manufacturers and crafters alike, desperate for brighter, more durable pigments to work with.

Arsenic green found its way into almost every facet of Victorian life, from green wallpaper to ladies' gloves, ribbons to playing cards, dress fabrics to children's toys. Fake flowers were sprayed with arsenic, wool was dipped in arsenic, hats were dyed with arsenic, and arsenic was even added to cosmetics, food and drink.

And yet, incredibly, the Victorians already knew arsenic was poisonous. Dubbed 'inheritance powder' for its use as a murderer's slow but deadly poison, arsenic was also a well-known rat killer and toxin. Even when medical journals and newspapers ran shocking accounts of the damage done by arsenic poisoning, few people listened. Hundreds of children died from exposure to arsenic wallpaper on nursery walls, women came out in blisters from tainted fabrics, and workers in pigment factories dropped like flies. Queen Victoria reportedly had all the green paper ripped from the walls of Buckingham Palace after a visiting official became ill.

One person to emerge badly from the arsenic scandal was philanthropist and Arts & Crafts founder William Morris. Morris, who had benefitted as a shareholder from the arsenic mining industry and became well-known for his hand-printed wallpaper, was famously dismissive of its suspected health effects, writing in 1885, 'As to the arsenic scare, a greater folly is hardly possible to imagine: the doctors were being bitten by witch fever.'

SILICA

There's a particularly nasty condition known as 'Potters' Rot'. Caused by inhaling silica dust, its modern name is silicosis and its symptoms include lung disease, fever and cyanosis (blue skin).

People have been making POTTERY (pages 124-129) for thousands of years. Working with wet clay is fine, but as soon as it dries or is fired, clay dust becomes dangerous to breathe in. Lots of parts of the pottery-making process create this dust, from scraping and brushing fired pots to simply being around clay as it dries.

In 1840, the House of Commons commissioned an enquiry. One interview with a scourer (someone who brushes fired pottery to remove loose material) in Stoke-on-Trent revealed 'It is so dusty it makes one short of breath; every one that works in this place suffers more or less with coughs, and we are all stuffed up; we have known a great many deaths from it; William Benley, who stands by me, has been 17 years in the place, and he knows five women who have died from it.'

Silica dust is also an occupational hazard of other crafts and industries, including mining, foundry work, STONEMASONRY (pages 156-157), tilemaking, brick making and GLASSMAKING (pages 144-145). Around the world around 50,000 people a year still die from the condition.

FURTHER READING

CRAFT PHILOSOPHY

Cræft: An Inquiry into The Origins and True Meaning of Traditional Crafts (2018), Alexander Langlands

Making Things Right: A Master Carpenter At Work (2015), Ole Thorstensen

The Architecture of Happiness (2006), Alain De Botton

The Case For Working With Your Hands: Or Why Office Work is Bad for Us and Fixing Things Feels Good (2010), Matthew Crawford

The Craft Reader (2009), Glenn Adamson

The Craftsman (2008), Richard Sennett

The Culture of Craft: Status and Future (1997), Peter Dormer

The Invention of Craft (2013), Glenn Adamson

The Nature and Art of Workmanship (2007), David Pye

Why We Make Things & Why It Matters (2017), Peter Korn

CRAFT REFERENCE

Amateur Craft: History and Theory (2015), Stephen Knott

Bronze (2012), David Ekserdjian and Cecilia Treves

Craft in America: Celebrating Two Centuries of Artists and Objects (2007), Jo Lauria and Steve Fenton

The Craft Industries (1972), J. Geraint Jenkins

Glass: A Short History (2012), David Whitehouse

Global Clay: Themes in World Ceramic Traditions (2017), John A. Burrison

Jewelry: From Antiquity to the Present (1996), Clare Phillips

Knitting: Fashion, Industry, Craft (2012), Sandy Black

Lost Crafts: Rediscovering Traditional Skills (2009), Una McGovern

Metalworking Through History: An Encyclopedia (2009), Ana Lopez

Paper: Paging Through History (2017), Mark Kurlansky

Paper Cutting (2011), edited by Laura Heyenga

Paper Making: The History and Technique of an Ancient Craft (1947), Dard Hunter

7000 Years of Jewellery (2007), Hugh Tait

Stitches In Time: The Story of the Clothes We Wear (2016), Lucy Adlington

Textiles: The Art of Mankind (2012), Mary Schoeser

The Art and History of Calligraphy (2017), Patricia Lovett

The Book: A Cover-to-Cover Exploration of the Most Powerful Object of Our Time (2016), Keith Houston

The Book Of Forgotten Crafts: Keeping The Traditions Alive (2011), Paul Felix, Sian Ellis & Tom Quinn

The Button Box: The Story of Women in the 20th Century, Told Through the Clothes They Wore (2017), Lynn Knight

The Forgotten Arts & Crafts (2001), John Seymour

The Lure of Gold: An Artistic and Cultural History (2006), Hans-Gert Bachmann

The Oxford Companion to the Decorative Arts (1975), edited by Harold Osborne

The Pot Book (2015), Edmund de Waal

The Secret Lives of Colour (2016), Kassia St Clair

The Story Of Craft: The Craftsman's Role in Society (1981), Edward Lucie-Smith

World Textiles: A Concise History (2003), Mary Schoeser

World Textiles: A Sourcebook (2012), Diane Waller

CRAFT ORGANISATIONS

100% DESIGN
100percentdesign.co.uk
The UK's biggest trade event for design, innovation and emerging craft talent.

AMERICAN CRAFT COUNCIL
craftcouncil.org
Leading US non-profit, organisation interested in cultivating a culture of craft and making.

BRITISH CRAFT TRADE FAIR
bctf.co.uk
Showcases the best of British craft – a useful and innovative shop window on UK talent.

CANADIAN CRAFTS FEDERATION
canadiancraftsfederation.ca
Empowering the professional contemporary craft sector through collaborative action and community development.

COCKPIT ARTS
cockpitarts.com
An award-winning UK creative business incubator for craft makers and social enterprise.

CRAFT CENTRAL
craftcentral.org.uk
A London-based home to studios, workspace, hot-desking, events space and more.

CRAFT COURSES
craftcourses.com
Online portal for creative, craft and artisan courses across the UK.

CRAFT IN AMERICA
craftinamerica.org
A non-profit US organisation whose mission is to promote original handcrafted work, through educational programmes and research.

CRAFT NORTHERN IRELAND
craftni.org
Supports and promotes the craft industry as a vibrant part of the region's economic and cultural infrastructure.

CRAFT SCOTLAND
craftscotland.org
The national development agency supporting makers and promoting craft.

CRAFT SPACE
craftspace.co.uk
Charity who creates opportunities for people to see and make contemporary craft. They build relationships between crafters and organisations, encouraging the sharing of skills and knowledge.

CRAFTIVIST COLLECTIVE

craftivist-collective.com

An activist social enterprise which uses 'craftivism' (craft and activism) to engage people in social justice issues and critical thinking.

CRE8TIME

cre8time.com

A US movement who promote the importance of creative expression and provide a forum for crafters to share their experiences with the wider creative community.

CREATIVE INDUSTRIES COUNCIL

thecreativeindustries.co.uk

A joint forum between the creative industry and UK government. Focuses on craft as a business with information on access to finance and intellectual property.

ETSY

etsy.com

An online marketplace for handmade and one-off craft items including clothing, textiles, ceramics and toys.

EUROPEAN FOLK ART AND CRAFT FEDERATION

europeanfolkartandcraft.com

A network of non-profit associations protecting and supporting traditional and contemporary crafts. Includes: (Austria) Kuratorium Österreichisches Heimatwerk; (Denmark) FORA Association for Adult Learning; Estonian Folk Art and Craft Union; The Finnish Crafts organization Taito; Hungarian Heritage House; Hungarian Folk Artist Association; The Association Latvian Folk Art Union; Norwegian Folk Art and Craft Association; (Poland) The Foundation Cepelia, Polish Art and Handicraft; (Serbia) Ethno Network; (Slovakia) Centre for Folk Art and Craft; and Swedish Handicraft Society.

FIFE CONTEMPORARY ART & CRAFT

fcac.co.uk

Contemporary visual art and craft organisation providing exhibitions and artist support.

FOLKSY

folksy.com

Online marketplace for British-made craft and design.

GREEN CRAFTS INITIATIVE

craftscotland.org/about/projects/green-crafts-initiative

Nationwide accreditation scheme designed to provide Scottish-based makers and craft organisations with advice, support and tools to become more sustainable and eco-friendly.

HANDMADE IN BRITAIN

handmadeinbritain.co.uk

Supports and promotes design and craft talent through fairs, events and pop-ups. Workshops and business mentoring to support designer-maker communities.

HERITAGE CRAFT ALLIANCE

heritagecraftalliance.co.uk

UK organisation who deliver heritage skills training and qualifications, working with organisations such as the National Trust and The Prince's Foundation.

LONDON CRAFT WEEK

londoncraftweek.com

Celebrates British and international creativity from established and emerging makers, designers and galleries from around the world.

MAKER SPACES

spaces.makerspace.com

An online, worldwide directory of spaces for makers.

MAKERS GUILD IN WALES

makersguildinwales.org.uk

Established in 1984 as a maker co-operative, the Makers Guild in Wales, UK brings together and promotes the best of Welsh craft talent.

MAKING SPACE

makingspace.org

A community-based craft organisation that creates opportunities for people to discover and develop design and making skills; increasing personal wellbeing through involvement in high-quality craft.

NATIONAL ASSOCIATION FOR THE VISUAL ARTS (NAVA)

visualarts.net.au

National body who protect and promote the professional interests of the Australian craft and design sector.

NATIONAL CENTRE FOR CRAFT AND DESIGN

nccd.org.uk

The largest venue in England dedicated to the exhibition and promotion of national and international craft and design.

NEW DESIGNERS

newdesigners.com

A two week UK exhibition celebrating and showcasing the creative future with over 3,000 breakthrough designers graduating.

THE CRAFTS COUNCIL

craftscouncil.org.uk

The national development agency for contemporary crafts in the UK. Online directory of makers, studio spaces, funding and craft projects.

THE CRAFTS STUDY CENTRE

csc.uca.ac.uk

An international centre for research in modern craft, museum collections and archives.

THE DESIGN TRUST

thedesigntrust.co.uk

Online business school for designers
& makers. Start, run and grow your craft
business through online workshops,
courses & blogs.

THE DEVON GUILD
OF CRAFTSMEN

crafts.org.uk

Acclaimed British exhibition space for
contemporary craft and design as well
as a leading charity for craft education.

THE HERITAGE
CRAFTS ASSOCIATION

heritagecrafts.org.uk

Advocacy body for traditional heritage
crafts – also provides details of makers,
grants and craft guilds.

THE NEW CRAFTSMEN

thenewcraftsmen.com

Curates, commissions and sells
contemporary craft including furniture,
lighting, textiles and ceramics by
UK makers.

THE WOMEN'S INSTITUTE

thewi.org.uk

From beginner makes to more advanced
techniques, community and charitable
projects, groups and workshops – UK
based crafting activities to suit all abilities.

WORLD CRAFTS
COUNCIL EUROPE

wcc-europe.org

Non-profit organisation who promote crafts
as an integral part of society's cultural,
social and economic wellbeing.

INDEX

ABOUT THE AUTHOR

Sally Coulthard is a best-selling author who has written over twenty books on interiors, decor, craft, rural life and traditional skills including *STUDIO: Creative Spaces for Creative People* (Jacqui Small), *How to Build a Shed* (Laurence King), and *The Little Book of Building Fires* (Anima). Brought up in a household passionate about craft, Sally went on to read Archaeology & Anthropology at Oxford University where she got hooked on the history of making. A passionate house-restorer and garden designer, she now divides her time between writing about stuff and making it.

ACKNOWLEDGEMENTS

A huge thank you to: **Harriet Butt**, editor
extraordinaire and all-round good egg;
Maeve Bargman, genius book designer;
Louise Lockhart for her extraordinarily
beautiful illustrations; **my parents**, for their
insights and attitude towards craft; and
my wonderful agent **Jane Graham Maw**.
This book has been an utter pleasure to
research and write, mostly because it's put
me in touch with dozens of hugely talented
crafters and artisans, who primarily make
stuff because it matters.

MALPAS